# THE ORIGINS OF DEMOCRATIC-SOCIALISM IN ISRAEL:
## FOUNDATIONS AND LEADERSHIP

**Ivan C. Frank, Ph.D.**

1

# TABLE OF CONTENTS

# ACKNOWLEDGEMENTS

First and foremost I want to thank my wife, Malke who showed great patience with my long hours of working on this project.

My own editors were Kate Murtaugh and Michael Bagen who diligently corrected errors and made excellent recommendations to make this book more readable. There were many friends and knowledgeable colleagues who helped me find books which I sought, contributed a book, or an article from their own collection, or an idea such as Ken Bob of Ameinu, Rabbi Jamie Gibson of Temple Sinai in Pittsburgh, Dr. Henry Near and Gary Ben-Et of Kibbutz Bet Ha-Emek. I also received valuable information and support from the staff at Y.I.V.O., The Jewish Research Institute, the Labor Zionist Executive Committee in Pittsburgh, the members of the Steering Committee of J Street in Pittsburgh, and from the staff of the Carnegie Library of Pittsburgh.

Lastly, but never least, I want to thank our son Ayal and daughter Michal who grew up in Israel, and always supported me during the writing of this book.

Ivan C. Frank, Ph.D.
Pittsburgh, PA.
March 6, 2011

# FORWARD

The goal of this book, The Origins of Democratic-Socialism in Israel, is to provide three different areas of description and analysis. First, I will describe and analyze the leadership of the first three Aliyot (Waves of Immigration to Israel) from 1880-1924. Second, we will explore the personal lives of the democratic-socialist leaders. Finally, we will review the names and stories of certain young people whose names are not famous, but who also made that leap across the sea in order to settle in the barren, desolate land of Palestine.

We will begin with the lives of the young pioneers, whose education, as well as the revolutionary conditions in Eastern Europe, influenced their pioneering spirit. We will discuss their ideological, political, and spiritual leadership, their ideological conflicts and compromises. I will also discuss the growth of the collectives and the settlement society, which the leadership helped to stimulate intellectually and spiritually.

The socialist and democratic foundations of the Jewish Palestinian settlement society developed with the support of the Zionist movement, the spiritual and physical attachment to the land of the young pioneers from Eastern Europe, and the institutions of the settlement society created from 1904-1924. These self-sufficient collectives arose with the assistance of the Zionist Movement and the Jewish National Fund, whose representative Arthur Ruppin arrived in Palestine in 1907 in what was the beginning of the movement toward self-sufficient agricultural settlements.

During the early Twentieth Century (1905-1924), famous *kvutzot* (plural of kvutza: the small collectives originally of ten to twelve men and women), were all established. They *kibbutzim* included(*plural of kibbutz*) such as Sejera, Ein Ganim, Kineret, Degania Aleph, Ein Harod, Merchavia, and Ayelet ha-Shachar; the organization of the Kibbutz Movement; Gedud ha-Avodah (The Labor Battalion).

As Amos Elon wrote in *The Israelis: Founders and Sons,*

There were leaders in 1968 in their eighties who had been resolute and resourceful when they worked for the Jewish people abroad, but at home

5

fought one another with a ferocity that seems to characterize the in-fighting of most revolutions. In their lifetime, historical processes normally much longer had shortened sensationally. In one short lifetime, a modern welfare state had grown up in what had been a backward barren thinly populated Ottoman province. They had lived their Utopias in their own lives (Elon 12-13).

It is that short history, the lives of the workers, and the leadership that I will focus on and analyze in the following pages.

My personal commitment to this topic of modern Jewish settlement in Israel stems from my having worked in Kibbutz Kfar Blum as a member of Habonim, the Labor Zionist Youth Movement, from 1957-1958, and in Kibbutz Nachal Oz with my family from 1977-1982. My mother's family didn't settle in Palestine, but left Odessa soon after the Bolshevik Revolution of 1917. They arrived first in Canada and later in the United States. This was time of the Second Aliyah, when the vast majority of Jewish immigrants arrived to Palestine (1904-1919). The minority of my mother's teenage peer group had organized themselves between the March 1905 Revolt and the 1917 Bolschevik revolution into a secret society with the intention to emigrate from Russia to the Ottoman Province.

My wife Malke and I were among the original members of the unique seed group Garin, recognized by the Jewish Agency as a settlement group as *Kvutzat* SHAAL. This group immigrated to the development town of Karmiel. We envisaged our seed group as an experiment to live in a democratically–organized urban collective, and were recognized by both the United Kibbutz Movement, *T.A.K.A.M.* (*Tnua ha Kibbutzit ha-Meuchedet*) and the Israeli socialist institutions of the *Histadrut ha-Klalit*.

While living in Israel, I wrote my dissertation (1981): a case study of at-risk youth from south Tel Aviv who were rehabilitated in a kibbutz Youth Aliyah program. In the 1990s, I completed two books describing how the ideology of the *kibbutzim* was prominent in the utilization of long-range programs that enabled counselors and teachers to rehabilitate at-risk youth from poor urban areas (*Children in Chaos* and *Building Self-Esteem in At-Risk Youth*). In those particular studies, the ideological setting of a kibbutz was a major factor in the rehabilitation of nineteen juvenile delinquents. During the time I was doing my research (1977-1982), I was a member in Nachal Oz, a kibbutz two kilometers from Gaza City. In that kibbutz, I periodically worked in the services and agriculture, but spent most of my time in the Regional College of the Negev and Ben Gurion University as a lecturer, an educational coordinator at the College of the Negev and Ben Gurion University, and as Educational Coordinator of the kibbutz. I also organized a seminar on "the situation" of the *kibbutzim*.

In the early 1980s, there was already much concern regarding the future of the Kibbutz Movement. Economic downturns and the weakening of the voluntary idealism of its founders had brought in many cases the economic viability of a number of *kibbutzim* into question.

Another area of concern was that after army service, 40% of the sons and daughters were leaving the kibbutz. Many of the veterans and the youth realized that the economic stability of the kibbutz and their own individual material well-being was endangered.

Since that time, there have been major social and economic changes in kibbutz ideology and organization. Some kibbutz members believe that in most ways their democratic government, socialistic planning or basic equality have not changed. As such, the kibbutz movement refers to these changes as 'renewal', not 'privatization' (Kirshner A. 1).

I have been involved in numerous discussions with kibbutz historians and studied the kibbutz movements at various times between the years 1957 and 1982. In that time I've taken note of how the democratic socialism of the first three *Aliyot* (1880-1924) influenced the members' ideology, and their personal contributions to the kibbutz, *kvutza*, or *moshav[1]*. I've discussed this with veterans of the kibbutz movement, many of them who've lived in the Jezreel Valley and the western or northern Galilee. They have included original leaders of Degania such as Joseph Baratz, who wrote the well-known book, *Village by the Jordan*; Eddie Parsons was an ideologist from Kfar Blum in the northern Galilee; Yehuda Schuster was the Director of the College of the Negev and a member of Kibbutz Mefalsim in the northern Negev; Yaakov Oved was a well-known expert on kibbutz life. There are other kibbutz veterans whom I've held discussions with more recently, such as Henry Near, the author of the two volume work: *The Kibbutz Movement*.

To this day, Israel is a welfare state, and its socialist elements are recognized as such by the Socialist International. The first settlements of the 1920's, the Labor Movement, and eventually the democratically governed Socialist-Zionist institutions, laid the framework for the democratic and socialist sector that arose in 1948 to compete with the capitalist sector. After the amalgamation of the Second and the Vienna Socialist Internationals in

---

1 Small holders cooperative village in which they lived.

May 1923, the newly formed Socialist International accepted the membership of the Poale Zion Confederation into the Socialist International, giving it two votes at its Convention. In 1929, after the union of the two labor parties in Palestine, *Ha-Poel ha-Tzair* and *Poale Zion*, the Labor Party of Palestine (*Mapai*) was recognized as the Jewish Section of the Labor and Socialist International in Palestine. It was also the only Palestinian labor party affiliated with the International (*The Socialist International and Zionism* 16-17).

Although the collective arrangements that were its classic element have declined, the kibbutz still has many features of basic equality. In some cases, such as in Kibbutz Geva and forty others, according to some historians, kibbutzim remain very much within the collective tradition. Israel's traditionally democratic conduct in governing, the early kibbutz movement's equality, and the social values of those pioneers to a large extent still exist. Thus, it is important to comprehend why and how the first three Aliyot occurred, and how the socialist leadership laid the foundation in the communal societies.

This settlement was accomplished with the important assistance of the Jewish Agency, The Jewish National Fund, (*Keren Kayemet*), the Palestine Foundation Fund (*Keren ha-Yesod*), and later the Land Development Authority. To a much lesser extent, early support came from a few prominent rabbis and Zionist leaders inside Palestine and in the Diaspora, men and women who helped lay the groundwork for an independent Democratic-Socialist Jewish State in Palestine.

The World Jewish Community and the Israeli nation are now focused on security, internal civil conflicts, and economic growth in the Jewish State. However, without the first three *Aliyot*, and the dominant Socialist-Zionist leadership (particularly in the second), the tiny state could not have achieved the social, economic, and political foundation and security apparatus to defend this land which the Jewish National Fund and the Zionist Movement purchased for communal settlements.

Therefore, the major goals of this book are: one, creating a clear picture of who were the leaders of the socialist movements, their characters and the Jewish background from which they and their followers in Palestine came; two, describing the conditions of the Eastern European Jews from 1880-1917; three, analyzing the revolutionary social movements which influenced their socialistic approach to settling the land and the democratic nature of their daily lives in Palestine; and four, explaining how young pioneers settled as farmers and urban proletariat in Palestine, developing the *kvutza*, the kibbutz and the

8

*moshav* (small holders cooperatives); and during the Third Aliyah (1919-1924); the *Histadrut*.

My research included original essays by leaders of the Second Aliyah, biographical and autobiographical information of more than a half dozen Socialist-Zionists, including Aleph Dalet Gordon, Berl Katznelson, Yitzchak Tabenkin, David Ben Gurion, Manya Shohat, Dov Ber Borochov, and Nachman Syrkin; from various sources which I discovered at the Farband Labor Zionist Library in Pittsburgh, the Carnegie Library in Pittsburgh, and Y.I.V.O, the well-known Yiddish Research Institute in New York City. I have read articles and pamphlets in Hebrew and Yiddish, and pored over the wealth of information in the books that my father-in-law Z'L' (in blessed memory) Eddie Steinfeld left to my wife Malke and I. He was an original member of the Labor Zionist movement and certainly was an inspiration for me in the writing of this book. I have scoured books in Hebrew, Yiddish, and English that relate to the kibbutz movements, the political parties, the socialist institutions founded and developed during the period of the first three waves of immigration, and the leadership of those settlements, political parties, and movements.

In many cases, my sources were individual writers who were close to the Socialist-Zionists and the Settlement Movement at the time of the Second and Third *Aliyot*. In the 1920's, one of them traversed the country, visiting a particular kibbutz and describing it in detail (Ludwig Lewisohn in his book *Israel*). I have also gleaned the writings of Joseph Baratz who lived in Degania *Aleph*, as well as essays penned by A.D. Gordon, David Ben Gurion, Berl Katznelson, Rachel Yanait, and Manya Shohat, intellectual and spiritual giants of those times. These men and women not only lived in and helped establish the *kvutzot* and the *kibbutzim*, but also became the major leaders of the Settlement Society in Israel during the first three waves of immigration.

All the above sources, including my own (which I acquired in 1976 while working for the Afro-Asian Institute of the Histadrut), provided me with a deep entry into important recollections and many written facts. Using the above materials, I was able to delve into the impact of the leadership on the ideology of the Democratic-Socialist Settlement Movement, and the establishment of democratic-socialism in Palestine during the early decades of the Twentieth Century.

# INTRODUCTION

The major leaders of the Socialist-Zionist Movement in Palestine, Aleph Dalet Gordon, Dov Ber Borochov, Manya Shohat, Berl Katznelson, Yitzchak Tabenkin and David Ben Gurion influenced the ideological, political, and spiritual lives of the members of the Settlement Society during the three immigration waves to Palestine, 1880-1924 (Of course there were other periods of immigration to Palestine dating back at least 1200 years). Due to his major role in the development of the Socialist Settlement Society, I made mention of Arthur Ruppin, the brilliant German sociologist of the Jewish National Fund who helped develop the model for agricultural self-sufficiency, as well as others who supported the cause of settling the land. The Jewish National Fund leased the land to the settlements so that it remained collectivized, and thus the J.N.F. prevented land speculation. Ruppin was one of the creators of the model settlement Degania *Aleph* I, the famous first kibbutz, and other collective settlements. Degania's model was one of the socialist and democratic decision-making types of collective settlements into which all *kvutzot and kibbutzim* evolved. (The *kvutzot* originally consisted of only ten to twelve members living in a special type of socialist collective during the Second Wave of immigration 1905-1919, and *kibbutzim* that was the name given to larger collective permanent settlements toward the beginning of the Third Wave of immigration to Israel).

I have also addressed the role of women in democratic socialist activism. Rachel Yanait and Manya Shohat established the Women's Workers Movement in 1915, and helped launch the Women's Workers Council in 1921.

In the last decades of the Nineteenth Century, the assistance of one Orthodox rabbi who supported the First Aliyah and was one of the founders of *Hovevei Zion* (the Lovers of Zion Movement) did play a role. Samuel Mohilever's role is important in terms of his encouraging the support of the settlements that attempted the first social experiments of the Settlement Movement from 1882-1903.

Although the *Kadima* (*Forward*) movement, so named by Peres Smolenski and using the major Zionist ideology of Leon Pinsker from his book *Auto-Emancipation*, was only a nationalist movement to fight Anti-Semitism on campuses in Vienna, after the Pogroms of 1882 in Eastern Europe (the Ukraine, Rumania, and Poland), it was the first group which put out a welcoming hand to Theodore Herzl (Gottheil 147-148).

Theodore Herzl, and Leon Pinsker are usually mentioned as the first two highly influential Zionist thinkers to encourage the Jewish population of Europe should eventually evacuate to Palestine. "Herzl had excited the imagination of the Jewish masses in the Russian Pale of Settlement, (the restricted areas where Jewish population could live in Eastern Europe) by a dream of Jewish statehood" (Eban 257). This occurred despite the Jewish religious authorities' opposition and declarations against it, including Orthodox rabbis, the Reform Movement Jewish "Church", as Goththeil called it, the more secular Jewish Colonization Association, the Alliance Unverselle of Paris as well as the Western groups of Hovevei Zion. The Reform Movement, as all Jewish religious denominations did, opposed Zionist settlement on the land in Palestine since they saw it as nationalism in opposition to their classical view of Judaism as a religion. The declaration of the Association of Rabbis in Germany in 1897 stated clearly..." that any attempts of the Zionists to found a Jewish national state in Palestine are contrary to the Messianic promises of Judaism..."(Gottheil 104).

However, the famous First Zionist Congress in 1897 in Basle did open. It was there that discussions about the Social Transformation of the Jewish people, and Zionism began a new chapter of Zionism and modern Jewish history.

Herzl, who had not dreamed of being the leader of a movement, had become the leader of Political Zionism and was the prime mover of that Congress (Zionism 95-105). However, at the extremes were the Political and Practical Zionists, and there was a great deal of stereotyping of both of them, which was a misfortune. The Political Zionists wanted an agreement first and colonization later, but the Practical Zionists hoped to settle the land without political agreements first; in other words, to establish facts on the ground. Only the extremists of Practical Zionism wanted the whole Hovevei Zion Movement to be transferred to Palestine. On the other side, the extremists of the Political Zionists felt that the colonization attempts were trivial (Gottheil 151-152).

Although Chaim Weizmann, the well-known first President of Israel and a prominent diplomatic Zionist, did not have a direct effect on the Jewish

11

democratic socialism of the settlement movement, he did come from the Russian Pale, he was "faithful to its values and pieties" (Eban 257).

Weizmann, who was the chief executive of the Jewish Agency, not only negotiated with Churchill and other officials of the Palestinian British Mandate Agency after 1917, but he also took part in many discussions before the end of World War I. He helped influence the British to create the Balfour Declaration, which foresaw a Jewish homeland in Palestine. Although he never worked on the land, he believed that the Jewish people should settle it. In his speech at the Eighth Zionist Congress in 1907, Weizmann said in part, "Our diplomatic work is important, but it will gain in importance by our actual accomplishments in Palestine" (The Jewish National Fund 16). Ben Gurion, the Chairman of the Vaad Leumi (the National Committee), the outstanding Jewish Agency figure who was the sole representative of the Jewish Agency to the British Government, the Secretary of the Histadrut (General Federation of Labor), and the political leader of the Settlement Society collaborated with him on a regular basis. Berl Katznelson a major socialist ideological leader and the closest political person to David Ben Gurion, also admired Weizmann and considered him the foremost Zionist of his day, a man of profound political comprehension (Shapira 173).

By 1924, the year denoting the end of the Third Aliyah, under Ben Gurion's direct leadership and with the assistance of a few socialist colleagues such as Berl Katznelson, the urban and rural Jewish pioneers of Palestine represented a new spirit in the country. The salient feature of modern Jewish society had become socialist and democratic in that spirit.

Haim Greenberg, an important Labor Zionist leader whose writings influenced Zionism and Socialism, Nachman Syrkin, and Joseph Haim Brenner (whose pen was sharp and who carried the image of ideological leadership), played relevant roles in the development of Democratic-Socialism in Palestine. However, due to illness, Brenner never worked the land. In one of Brenner's famous Hebrew novels, Mi-Kan Umi Kan (From Here and There,) the elderly Tolstoyan hero A.D. Gordon is featured. In that novel, Ariyeh Lapidot, the hero, and his grandson collect thorns for fire to bake bread. "The old man and the youth were both crowned by thorns, as they stood the watch of life together." Thus, Joseph Brenner was describing the Second Aliyah the Second Wave of immigration to Palestine, 1905-1919, during which the famous collectives, kvutzot and kibbutzim were established. Brenner, who was a member of the Poale Zion political party (Workers of Zion) by 1911, was describing the nearly impossible lives of the Second Aliyah (www.Zionism-Israel.com 1-3).

Therefore, the ideas of such well-known Zionists figures who were socialists, but did not lead communal or collective lives on the land, will be highlighted at times; especially when it is apparent that their ideas influenced the building of the foundations of a Socialist-Zionist State, the Settlement Society, the Watchmen (ha-Shomer), The Labor Bataliion, (Gedud ha-Avodah) the *Histadrut*, and the first two socialist political parties (*Poale Zion* and *Ha-Poel ha-Tzair*).

The women of the Second Aliyah while still preparing for aliyah in such cosmopolitan cities as Odessa, had been taught to expect full equality with men, but later found themselves in the kibbutz doing only domestic labor. Those expectations of the women, who were twenty percent of the Second Aliyah, were not always realized and created in them the motivation to establish their own movement. They were determined to reach those expectations (Fuchs 6-7). Equality in the context of the late Nineteenth and early Twentieth Centuries, however, did not mean abolishment of the roles of women in relationship to men.

Female literary figures, such as Rachel Blaustein and Leah Goldberg, were involved politically in Palestine, and lived in the first kvutzot. Several such women leaders, and many others who looked for agricultural work, numbered 20% of the Second Aliyah, and did settle in a kvutza, a moshav (small holder cooperative in which each family had its own piece of land), or in a kibbutz. They expected to live in an egalitarian society alongside 'the new man' and play major roles. They left us with numerous poems that we still study and identify as the individualistic socialist literature of the Second Aliyah. During the Third Aliyah, women such as Shira Gorshman joined the radical Labor Battalion (Gedud ha-Avodah) whose members leased themselves to the British to work on roads or in the stone quarries. When it appeared that Palestine would not become deeply committed to the ideals of the Communist Party, the Labor Battalion split, and its left-wing faction with Shira and other women in tow moved to the Crimera where the Soviets were settling Jews in agricultural communes (Mniewski; Pollack 17).

Some of the women, such as Manya Shohat and Rachel Yanait became more active politically in the socialist society and were members of the Histadrut and labor leaders in their own rights. They also were in the Labor Battalion and the Watchmen (*ha-Shomer*). Their socio-economic and political roles are part of the dynamic in the development of the democratic-socialist society in Palestine

In modern Palestinian and Israeli history, one constant that has always existed has been the political and philosophical splintering of the various parties and movements to which the Second *Aliyah* in particular had participants who were loyal. This phenomenon continued once the British Mandate ended in 1948, and stretched into the 1977 election of Menachem Begin, the leader of the right-wing Likud party. Of course, it still exists in Israel today. Without my attempting to emphasize that element, it does need to be highlighted in this book, since it does play an essential role in the development of the modern Zionist democratic-socialist revolution in Palestine.

It is incumbent upon me to add that one cannot easily distinguish between the leadership and their followers in the Settlement Society from 1880-1924, and the Jewish political party leaders and Labor Movement leaders after Israel became independent in 1948. There were always some leaders who created the splinter groups, some who only wished there would be unity; and there were always loyal followers of both types of leaders.

Whether the reader deems himself or herself a democratic socialist or not, I hope that the maximum effort he or she makes will go toward understanding the roots, the true conditions, the ideology, and the development of the democratic-socialist settlement movement in Palestine from 1880-1924. It had an enormous impact on the establishment of the State in 1948, and to this day on the present day discussions and direction the State is taking.

At the time that Zionist thinkers as Theodore Herzl, the Budapest-born reporter who wrote *The Jewish State* (He had witnessed Anti-Semitism at the Dreyfus Trial), Leo Pinsker, Moses Hess, Max Nordau, and Leib Lilienblum were preaching and seeking Jewish national redemption through early modern Zionist theories, ideology, and world–wide diplomatic efforts in the late Nineteenth Century, others were preparing themselves to make *aliyah* and live on the land in Palestine.

The expectations of the settlers who wrote about their ideology and daily living compose one of the major themes of this book. However, not only did the intellectuals and prominent political leaders have expectations, but so did many other young men and women in the early decades of the Twentieth Century. Although they all did not write articles and essays for the party newspapers, or the socialist institutions, they carried in their own hearts the expectations of living their idealism in Palestine. In our own time, there are still many ideologists who are writing about Israel, and their Zionist expectations. They certainly consider themselves to be believers in the democracy and the need of social justice in the Jewish State.

In terms of the earlier expectations, a quote of Haim Nachman Bialik will suffice as one introduction. In the 1920's, Bialik, the great Hebrew poet, upon hearing the news that there was a burglary for the first time in Tel Aviv ran joyously through the streets proclaiming the age-old benediction: "Blessed be He who has let us live to see this day and hour." Another interesting anecdote which describes the expectations of the chalutzim of first three Aliyot was told by Rachel Yanait, who married the second President, Yitzchak Ben-Zvi. This one illustrates the point. At the depth of the Great Depression, Ben Gurion was bitterly reproached by one of the unemployed. "Why are you complaining?" he replied. "Don't you feel good? How can you not feel good in our land?" (He was offering the only thing he could–the Zionist dream which was for the idealists as he was an expectation of a Jewish Socialist homeland in Eretz Israel (Near 133).

Later, in 1947-1948, there was the rapturous prediction on the occasion of the emergence of the state by those who were convinced that the achievement of the impossible would be a routine daily and unfailing phenomenon. In the early decades of the Twentieth Century, there were many Jews who had their own private and ecstatic expectations that Israel would be the perfect socialism of tomorrow, hardened by the stern rock of Marx, but sweetened by the balm of David Ben Gurion, and Berl Katznelson.

Haim Greenberg and Dov Ber Borochov, Labor Zionists who helped create the Socialist Zionist ideology of the early Twentieth Century warned against assimilation in Russia and even in America. Some Jews were deploring the emergence of such a state as a puppet of the Kremlin or a chauvinistic thorn in the side of Jewish communities abroad. This state would jeopardize Jewish security in countries in which had recently adopted them. These two Labor Zionist giants definitely reached the conclusion that there was not one European State in which the Promised Land could exist. David Ben Gurion who became the titular leader of the Mapai Labor party after 1930 and Berl Katznelson, the Socialist Zionist ideologist who preached unity, settling the land, and speaking Hebrew during the struggles leading up to the esatablishment of the State provided the pragmatic leadership in Palestine which drew the conclusions of Ber Borochov and Greenberg and developed the society which the theoretical Zionist Socialists envisaged.

15

The theorists who had advocated and supported the youthful Eastern European Jewish pioneers came from many different Zionist ideologies. They advocated why and how the Jewish people should come to live in Israel. In his *Rome and Jerusalem* (1862), Moses Hess, who Marx had taunted by calling him "that communist Rabbi Moses," believed in morality as a force equal to if not superior to materialism and had advocated for a Jewish national home in Palestine on the basis of social justice. Although a Spinozaist disposed to determinism, he was a humanist who clung to human nature as the dominant revolutionary factor in history. Unlike Herzl and even Leo Pinsker who had written the famous Zionist tract, *Rome and Jerusalem* in 1860, Hess claimed that the Jewish people needed a homeland to escape the pogroms and Anti-Semitism of Europe in the latter half of the Nineteenth Century. Hess placed the Holy Land at the heart and core of his philosophy. Palestine and Jerusalem were not just places on a map but the embodiment of his ideology. Moshe Leib Lilienblum, born in Russia in 1843 and known to some as "the Reformer," hoped and prayed for the continued existence of his people and to avert the tragedy of their likely extinction became a leading spirit of the *Hibath-Zion* (Lovers of Zion).

Religious Zionists as Smuel Mohilever, the head of the Vilna Yeshiva also expressed support for the First Aliyah settlers. Although he was an Orthodox Eastern European rabbi, a fervent believer in Religious Zionism, he was hopeful that the First Aliyah secular settlers would also succeed.

Nordau was a political Zionist. He also came to his Zionism because of European Anti-Semitism. He was a rationalist not a dreamer, but his spirited pen was used to fend off the attacks on Zionism of many a Reform rabbi who opposed settling on the land in Palestine since they associated with religious fervor. In his own speeches, he thundered against the injustices against his people. Many Zionists consider an equal to Herzl. It was he who told Herzl that the Jewish people needed a sovereign state in *Eretz Israel*, one recognized by the international community, but not necessarily a State in all of Israel. In that respect, he was a believer in a democratic society that would share the land with the Arab peoples who were already there.

It is relevant to the history of the Israeli early Twentieth Century social movement, its political democracy, and its socialist outlook to demonstrate its ideological continuity, so I will describe not only the Zionist and democratic-socialist expectations of the early leaders and the settlers of the three waves of immigration from 1880-1924, but also allow the reader to consider the expectations of the historians who wrote of the period of 1909 until the Second

16

World War, as well as the post-State (1948) prominent Socialist Zionists who are democrats and believe in the social justice values of the early pioneers. They are professors, writers, justices, and political personalities.

Schlomo Avineri, a well-known progressive Political Science professor at the Hebrew University is the author of the *Making of Modern Zionism*. David Grossman and Amoz Oz are two of the most popular Israeli writers today. Avram Burg is well-known ex-Knesset member who was a speaker of the Knesset, Daniel Friedmann is the present Justice Minister and Aaron Barak is the former Chief Justice of Israel's Supreme Court. The Spiritual Progressives of the Jewish community in the United States support a Jewish State in its efforts to synthesize universal democratic values with the particular need for political independence in the State of Israel, "the land we love and hold sacred and always longed for" which translates into the democratic and Zionist goals of the early Twentieth Century.

Leonard Fein, and Anne Roiphe are op-ed journalists for The Jewish Forward and the Jerusalem Report respectively and have written and spoken extensively about their expectations for the Jewish State of Israel. At one forum or another, and in one article or another, these prominent writers, justices, politicians, and professors who have ideals congruent with the democratic-socialist values of the early *chalutzim* ask whether we should expect the State to be normal like all others or an "exemplar of what human society can be" (Roiphe 47).

After she ably describes the State's many short comings in that article, Roiphe continues by stating that it has held its values dear, and somehow maintained peace between religious fundamentalism and the secular majority. Ms. Roiphe claims that in Israel, there are few sweatshops, few toxic dumps, and few products polluted with poisons.

Anne Roiphe is less critical at times than Schlomo Avineri, David Grossman, and Avram Burg the ex-speaker of the Parliament who wast criticized by the left wing for his revisionism. In mid-November, 2008, an article in the Israeli newspaper Haaretz emphasized that a new left-wing movement (The New Movement) that did develop a new party was having its first gathering under the leadership of MK Haim Oren of Meretz (The present day political party which is more left wing than the Labor Party). Those who planned to attend were well-known writers and poets, such as A. B. Yehoshua, Amoz Oz, Ronit Matalon, and Dorit Rabinyan, as well as Labor Party figures as Avraham Burg, Uzi Baram, Gilad Sher, Yossi Kucik, and Mordechai Kremnitzer.

It is inevitable that if such a movement would grow stronger as an important piece of a left wing movement, that New Movement will need to absorb what remains of the left-leaning Labor Party and Meretz that have been weakened in the last decade. The goal would be to revive the Democratic-Socialist bloc in the Parliament.

In regard to socio-political matters, it is logical that its expectations will be similar to those of scholars and writers such as Shlomo Avineri, David Grossman, and others who are members of the Green Party, as well as Diaspora Jews such as Leonard Fein and Anne Roiphe who have expressed the same socialist Zionist ideals.

In 1998, in the book, *Zionism, The Sequel*, Barbara Spectre writes that the three principles of Zionism, Democracy, and Judaism are not only compatible but also mutually supportive. They are linked for her to people, land, and God. She then announced that it would be a most gratifying assertion, if it could be justified. However, in our modern time with the expectations that she and others still hold, she saw her task as one to sharpen the discrepancies so that the subject could be discussed with integrity. In the 1950's, the Israeli Communists only adhered to democracy and were not interested in Judaism represented by the Torah and a belief in God; and the Zionists as represented by the extreme right-wing Kach movement, and more recently some of the *Gush Emunim* (The Bloc of the Faithful) West Bank settler leadership only considered the Jewish Homeland at the expense of ignoring democratic principles. Of course, the ultra-orthodox (*Haredi*) population in Israel did not accept anything but Torah and God. In summary, each group accepted only one of three principles (Spectre). In the same book, essayist Haim Be'er raises the issue of tradition versus the secular pioneering reality of the labor movement pioneers.

Muki Tzur a well-known teacher and historian of the Second and Third Aliyah, and other writers and poets such as Yosef Aharonovitch and Avraham Shlonsky ask questions and make statements which permeate the secular reality of the pioneers of the Second and Third *Aliyot*. For example, one of Muki Tzur's characters asks: "Was this (The Second Aliyah, 1905-1919) a break with tradition or a return to it" (Diament 199-200)?

The pioneers of the Second Aliyah (1905-1919) were as a worker named Luka said to Manya Shohat, "We are compost for the next generation" (Diament, 189-190). Democratic and socialist principles had to be established each day while on the Galilee land in *kvutzot* such as Kfar Giladi, 1916,

Kineret, 1913, and Ayelet Ha Shachar, 1918; they were eating bread and onions.

The first parties in Palestine created a Jewish political setting in which there was more ideological hair-splitting than was necessary, considering the difficult tasks ahead for the leadership. It was clearly characteristic, however, of Jewish cultural and political life, which never negated the democratic volunteerism of that time. In the end, the results in terms of democratic governance and socialism were positive and miraculous.

In The *Israeli Worker*, Dr. Ferdynand Zweig, a professor at the Hebrew University in the field of Labor Relations, agrees that it was both democratic and socialist aspirations, but adds that it was even more. He unequivocally stated: "It is not enough to say that Israel aspires to a democratic structure of society in its Western version, it is not even enough to say that it aspires to Western socialistic patterns of society. Israel aspires to something more or let us say to something different." He concludes that Israel strives to combine Western socialism with purely Jewish values, to infuse it with the spirit of Judaism, to mix Marx with the prophets; and in a final insightful remark, similar to one made in the classic *To The Finland Station a History of Socialism*, by Edmond Wolfe, Zweig exclaims "After all Marx was impregnated with the heritage of the prophets. He even looked like a Prophet" (Zweig 4).

After he describes how Israel is a mixture of old and new, and of the sacred and the profane, Zweig emphasizes his own utopian expectations: "Salvation will come to Israel only through toil and sweat, through the role of the *new working classes* (my *italics*) which are in the process *of* formation" (Zweig 3-4).

It is thus true that in his eyes and in the eyes of many scholars after the State was established in 1948, the Socialist-Zionist struggle was still occurring. The chalutzim who never would have dreamed that the State would arise in their own lifetimes certainly could envision the socialism of their expectations needing much more hard work to reach fulfillment. The 'redemption' was begun by them and the next two or three generations had to complete the task. It was the utopian goal in the Second and Third Aliyot to 'fulfill oneself' by 'conquering labor' (The popular Hebrew concepts Hagshama Atzmit and Kibbush Avodah even existed in the collective settlements in the 1960's). In Zwelg's own present time (1959), the goal had not changed.

19

In more recent times, younger writers such as J. J. Goldberg have been concerned with the undemocratic and racist approach and reactions of the citizenry and the lack of governmental consideration for minorities, such as the Ethiopian Falasha Mura and Israeli Arabs. "The Jewish State is turning into something its founders never intended, something that may not even be sustainable, and nobody has a clue about what to do about it"(Goldberg 6).

All the articles, speeches, and statements of these men and women advocate that Israel be a light unto the nations. All of them relate to Democratic and Socialist values with a special touch of Jewish tradition, and all of them refer directly or indirectly to the Jewish Settlement Movement of the early decades of the Twentieth Century in Palestine. Those expectations do represent many of the Jewish peoples' expectations today, whether they live in Israel or consider themselves modern Zionists living in the Diaspora.

From the tradition, there stands out the prophets, Isaiah, Micah, and Amos who loved Israel and were true socialists, and t their goals related more to justice when it came time to be mindful of the oppressed. The secular Twentieth Century Jewish radicals in Palestine propagated their own ideals based on those prophets' words. David Ben Gurion often claimed that Socialist-Zionism was based on those prophetic Socialist ideologies. The prophets, as Isaiah, said that God would comfort us (The Jewish people); and we would make the desert bloom. In our time, many professors, chief justices, and politicians, even if in not so many words, believe this is the future of Israel, not leaving it pure desert, and making great efforts to grow tomatoes.

# I

## INFLUENCE OF THE RUSSIAN REVOLUTIONARY MOVEMENTS ON IMMIGRATION TO ISRAEL, 1905-1917

*"If Marx is contemptuous of his race, it is primarily perhaps with the anger of Moses at finding the Children of Israel dancing before the Golden Calf"—From* To the Finland Station, *by Edmund Wilson*

There were a total of five million Jews in Russia and the adjacent lands of Austria, Hungary, and Romania. This was in spite of the death toll from pogroms following the 1880 assassination of Czar Alexander II of Russia. At this time there were also one million Jews living in the United States. The approximate percentage of Jews in Eastern Europe was 60-70% of the total Jewish population in the World. Jews were present during the Civil War between the Red Army of the Bolsheviks and the Whites (Monarchists, Ukrainians, Czechs, and even American troops at Archangel). Present in the hundreds of thousands, it follows that the political structure of Israel in the early Twentieth Century was based to a large extent on the influence of the liberal ideas of Nineteenth Century Eastern Europe.

The young Russian Jews of the Second Aliyah (1905-1919) were brothers and heirs to Russian intellectuals who were Mensheviks (not Leninists as some as Ben Gurion were described) (Tyler 29), members of the People's Will (Narodnaya Volya), or Social Revolutionaries whose souls were connected to the peasants (Berlin 150). During the period of the First Aliyah (immigration wave, 1880-1904), 25,000 of the Jewish idealists who wished to settle on the

21

land arrived in Palestine, but the goal of creating a self-sufficient agricultural society in that period never came to fruition.

However, in the Second Aliyah "the young people were inspired both by the Balfour Declaration which promised the Jewish people a home in Palestine (1917) and the Russian Revolution (1917) to believe that the world was on the eve of a new era, (and they) formed small groups which began to make their way to Palestine-at first spontaneously…"(Near 59).

In Berl Katznelson's student time, he was associated with circles of young Jews in White Russia and the Ukraine who were deeply affected by the pain of the people's disaster. This was in 1903, just after the destructive Kishinev Pogrom. Their mood was comprised of a sense of responsibility for the national destiny, and awareness of the obligations and awareness of their actions potentially monumental implications. Their pessimism caused him for one to remark, " We breathed the air of extinction." To rationalize their pessimism they evolved the theory of 'non-proletarization.' The essence of the theory, which Berl Katznelson also claimed himself as one of the authors, was the denial of the ability of the Jewish people in the Diaspora to make the transition from lumpen proletariat to true working class status (Shapira 13).

The latter theory also appeared in the writings of Nachman Syrkin and Dov Ber Borochov (Shapira 13; Zweig 44). In Bertram Wolfe's Three Who Made A Revolution Revolution, he has argued that many of those young Jews preferred to join their own Socialist or Socialist-Zionist party or remained politically uninvolved. Some of the leading Jewish ideologists such as Pavel Axelrod and Julius Martov of the Social Democrats played major roles in the Menshevik faction. These two leaders were the Mensheviks who broke with Lenin. Although they were the majority party from 1890-1917 when the Social Democratic Party was functioning, the Mensheviks were referred to as the minority faction. (Lenin, the leader of the Bolshevik faction decided to call the new party the Communist Party after his arrival in Russia in April, 1917) (Wolfe 473-474).

From the late Nineteenth Century until at least the Communist Revolution of 1917, young Jewish socialists identified with poor artisans, land laborers, and factory workers whose cause they fought. After the period of the Enlightenment of the late Eighteenth Century and early Nineteenth Century and during the Revolutions of 1848, the Jewish youth who had made their way to the cities of Russia became a natural constituency for radicalism, as they suffered both national and class oppression. At first, many of them tried to organize the Christian peasants, since their fellow Jews were hopelessly parochial, and the new radicals no longer lived in the tight-knit communities in which Jews were indoctrinated to fear non-Jews. Even in that *shtetl* community there was class warfare, since the poorer Jews were soaked by dues and fees imposed by the shtetl elite, and the poor youth sent to the Czarist army instead of the richer Jewish businessmen who bought their children's way out. However, the failure of the Revolution of 1905 created disillusionment, since it did not deliver the promised parliamentary democracy of the Duma. When the Czarist regime suppressed its efforts, the Jews of Russia began to consider emigration to Palestine as the solution.

Socialist-Zionism which began to crystallize both as an idea and a movement in 1897 reached its peak in Czarist Russia. At that time, there were 5 million Jews in Eastern Europe and within 386,000 square miles of the area where Jewish people could exist (The Russian Pale), 94% of that Jewish population lived. The leadership of the First Zionist Congress in that year discussed both Socialism and Zionism. At that time, Nachman Syrkin began to propagandize the Jewish Socialist State in a series of essays with a result that in 1904 originated the first Socialist Zionist group. Syrkin believed in working on political socialism in the Diaspora while "the proletariat Zionists organized the Jewish masses to force the assimilated bourgeoisie to aid in building up the national homeland" (*Labor Zionist Hand-book*).

In 1900, Socialist-Zionist groups were establishing themselves in various cities of the Pale without any organizational unity. They soon realized that, lacking a healthy Jewish proletariat and no Jewish ruling class, there wasn't a path for them in their struggle for socialism in the Diaspora. After the rejection of Uganda as a Jewish Homeland, which occurred in 1903-1904, the Zionist Socialist Party organized and became the strongest of the many Socialist-Zionist groups. They arrived at their ideology from a Marxian approach, but their activities centered on encouraging immigration, believing as they did that the course of Jewish immigration would automatically determine the "territory" of Jewish mass concentration. The non-Marxian Semists were in close contact with the Social Revolutionaries and sought national Jewish autonomy with a "parliament. Officially it was referred to as the Jewish Socialist Labor Party. After 1917, that party united with the Bund (a non-Zionist Labor party, translating from the Yiddish as "Jewish Labor Alliance") and the Communist Party. In southern Russia, however, under the leadership of Ber Borochov, Poale Zion united Russian Social Democracy with Zionism, and in 1906 the Jewish Social-Democratic Party or Poale Zion was officially established.

What distinguished the Poale Zion from the other groups was its insistence on Palestine as the territory of the future Jewish homeland (Labor Zionist Handbook 10). Ber Borochov's Russian Poale Zion program developed along the lines of Jewish immigrants needing to have economic activity which would allow them or force them to lose their industrial and commercial character; and Palestine was the country for them to settle, since it was not a highly industrial capitalist territory, nor an agriculturally rich country, but a semi-agricultural one with a transitional economy. Thus the planks of the Russian Poale Zion were (1) the maximum demand: the complete socialization of the means of production (2) the minimum demand: the establishment of territorial autonomy for the Jewish nation in Palestine along democratic lines and through the class struggle. (my italics) (11) In Degania, "the affairs of the kvutza were managed in an informal way and, on the whole egalitarian manner. Every evening, at a general discussion in which all could participate, the following days work was allocated" (Near 37). As has been noted, Degania was considered a model kvutza (In terms of numbers of settlers, twelve or under was the early numerical standard of the kvutza).

However, the abandonment of the Russian intelligentsia's revolutionary positions can not be clearly defined in terms of young Jews choosing their Jewish backgrounds and Zionism over the Russian Revolutionary Movement. Jews of the late Nineteenth and early Twentieth centuries had been subject to various claims of almost every doctrine or dogma from extreme orthodoxy in a variety of forms, through a half dozen forms of Zionism, and even to enlightenment and assimilation. Before 1905, as Russians, they had been influenced by anarchism from nihilism to Kropotkin-style communism, populism of the *Narodnaya Volya* variety, by Fourier and Tolstoyan thought, by nationalists as Mazzini and Herder, to the ideology the various social democratic parties of Bolshevism and Menshevism. In one of his letters to Hannah Arendt, the German Zionist leader Kurt Blumenfeld said that Zionism was "Europe's gift to its Jews" (Diament 303.) Thus they were caught on the two horns of the dilemma: the Jewish solution, and solving the problems of humanity as a whole (Near 13).

Jewish intelligentsia had begun joining revolutionary movements such as the Peoples Will (*Narodnaya Volya*) as early as the early 1880s. The attacks on the revolutionaries by Czarists after 1881 Assassination of Alexander II became anti-Semitic reactionary attacks organized by the officialdom. Although sometimes the pogroms were denounced by radically-minded individuals on both humanitarian and political grounds, the prevalent attitude in revolutionary circles was one of sympathy with the perpetrators, the peasants, and the lower classes (Yarmolinsky 294-295).

In the biography of Nachman Syrkin, Marie Syrkin states that for the Jewish *Narodnik*, the pogroms of 1881 were a shock in more ways than one. Not only did the noble peasants reveal an extraordinary willingness to be instigated by the Russian government, but the Executive Committee of the *Narodnaya Volya* issued a proclamation condoning the pogroms and inciting the peasants to further efforts" (Syrkin 38).

It is no wonder that the solution for the *chalutzim* was Socialism and Zionism with a certain democratic-Talmudic flavor at odds with the Jewish tradition that had sunk deeply into the consciousness of the *hederim* of Eastern Europe.

The Jewish Socialist-Zionist approach was never supported by the Yiddish speaking Bund, which also arose as a movement around the time of the First Zionist Congress (1897). Bund was originally affiliated with the Social-Democratic party, and with the proletarization of the Jewish masses, the Jewish social democrat had to reach out to the Jewish working class. Since Yiddish was the popular language of the Pale of Settlement, the movement that was launched was the Bund. Using Yiddish as a convenience, "Jewish workers were told to tear their narrow traditional ties and lose themselves in the liberation of humanity" (Syrkin 39).

However, the Bund had a different goal. Its main ideological position was to support the working class of all nations, and it viewed Zionism as a nationalist illusion. Bundists did not have a traditional Jewish education. The Marxist Plekhanov bitter gibe about the Bund as sea-sick Zionists was the reaction of Russian Marxism to the Bundist ideology. When Berl Katznelson, a leading Socialist-Zionist, and lieutenant of David Ben Gurion, went to America to raise monies for the Palestinian Bank, the Bundists would not help him. The Bolsheviks never accepted the Bund, and the Bund withdrew from its Social-Democratic affiliation once it observed the Bolsheviks opposition to national sections. The Bolsheviks also never recognized the Jews as a separate ethnic group. It was believed that the Leninists wanted to prove to the world that, and possibly to display the government's overall tolerance of, minority groups that never would fulfill their national aspirations. Lenin did not even bother to be anti-Semitic. In the early 1920's, it was assumed by Lenin that such national groups would quietly disappear from the scene.

In general, socialists in Europe did not sympathize with the Jewish plight. The Jewish Communists in America never even spoke about Palestine until 1934 when the "Popular Front" became the Communist Party's watchword. Only then could they say a kind word about Palestine. As it turned out, the Bund was driven out of Russia and later Poland, and the Jewish Socialist-Zionists decided the proletariat of Judaism would have to immigrate to Palestine.

After the Kishinev Pogrom (1903), the Socialists did not join in the major demonstration of the Jewish proletariat, even as the peasants and work men declined to make common cause with their Jewish fellow citizens. (Gottheil, 167) "In Germany and Austria, the Christian Socialists Party evidently intended to turn Socialists away from their international and anti-religious dreams, making their juncture with Jewish Laborers impossible" (*Zionism* 168).


On other hand, young intellectual Russian and Polish Jewish socialists who made aliyah and were members of Ha-Poel ha-Tzair (one of the two main parties which existed during the first decades of Jewish Palestinian settlement activity) believed it was establishing a Second Homeland (with the U.S.S.R. being the first). *Ha-Poel ha-Tzair's* ideology had felt the impact of Tolstoy's philosophy, the ideology of the Russian Social Revolutionaries, and the early social living patterns of the communal life of anti-materialistic and pure equality similar to that of the Essenes of the First Century C. E. As late as 1948, *Mapai*, David Ben Gurion's ruling Labor Party in the first Knesset (Parliament), and the more left-wing *Mapam* closely resembled the idealistic membership of the Mensheviks; but it had developed the Socialist-Zionist Party, whose members had understood that only in Israel could Jewish workers live a democratic and socialist Jewish life.

Shlomo Avineri, in his book *The Making of Modern Zionism, The Intellectual Origins of the Jewish State*, (November 1981, Basic Books, New York, NY) wrote: "some of Israel's socialism-that for example the kibbutz-owed more to Tolstoy than Marx" He also states a believe in Zionism as a "permanent revolution", which "created a new normative and public focus for Jewish existence continues to strive for a radically different and more nearly just society in Israel" (Dannhauser 1-2).

Joseph Brenner and A.D. Gordon, two of the main ideologues and spiritual leaders of the Second Aliyah, also believed, like Tolstoy, in returning to the land and conquering it. In any case, many of the pioneers to whom Avineri was referring joined The Labor Battalion. Many of the Labor Battalion members later returned to the U.S.S.R. and entered the Jewish autonomous collective in Birobidzhan to become Russian Jewish farmers. In a small Jewish museum in Saint Petersburg, one can find the lyrics of the song they sang ("Who said that Jews can not be farmers spit in their eyes who would so harm us"). This was taken from the Jewish song "Hey Zhankoya," which described life in the Jewish collective of Birobidzhan. As early as 1928, Stalin encouraged this Jewish collective. Although it was referred to as a Jewish autonomous region when it was settled in 1934, its Jewish inhabitants never exceeded 20% of the total population. It was completely dismantled in 1958 by Nikita Khruschev after he admitted its failure, which he blamed on Jewish individualism (Frank, Ben 82).

The U.S.S.R. was not receptive to an autonomous Jewish national territory, even if it was Marxist in ideology. Haim Greenberg, a well-known Labor Zionist once wrote in "Why Not Birobidzhan," "Can you imagine Jews living in a Soviet collective slave labor camp?" Jewish socialism had found a home in Palestine and Dov Ber Borochov and Nachman Syrkin amongst others had reached the correct conclusions. Jewish intellectuals could change the economic character of their lives in order to establish socialism in an autonomous Jewish territory which was semi-agricultural, if they socialized the means of production and lived in a communal way with a democratic form of governance (volunteerism was a key element in the Jewish means of governance in Palestine and in the early days of the young Israeli state).

In The Jewish Century, Yuri Slezkine pointed out that the three options available to Russian Jews at the turn of the Twentieth Century were Liberalism, Zionism, and Communism. Of these three, the third one was gone, and the first two were illegal. This made Moscow and Leningrad Jews unreliable and in some cases oppositional. In the later Soviet period, Western Liberalism and Zionism were predominately Jewish and entirely Jewish respectively. The Jews were urban intellectuals and the claim that even the Bolshevik Revolution had been Jewish to a considerable extent has carried only a degree of truth, as it has usually been dismissed by many well-known historical writers (Slezkine 341).

Many liberal Jews who rebelled were upset with Czarism, not because they were oppressed and treated like serfs, but because they felt equal to the

Czar and above the serfs. (Slezkine 339-340) However, David Ben Gurion in 1919 and the Sabras (Native Israeli born) of the 1930s and early 1940s viewed their Jewish Settlement Society in Palestine as a small, particularistic, and proudly parochial homeland. The social movement that the pioneers created included an ideological environment in the schools where literature was studied from an ethnocentric point of view, and the press that the sabras read was culturally ethnocentric. The curriculum of planners and teachers declared openly that the consciousness of the Sabra youth was cast in Zionist and Socialist ideology. In 1933, a third grade walk in the fields included "Why do we fertilize and how do we fertilize the land of Israel"? But unlike the Soviet Union, its ideological unity was entirely based on volunteerism. At the same time, they also they eschewed individualism.

Their ideology was as messianic as Marxism, but in Palestine, Jews were not rebels, nor were they oppositional. "It was messianic but also one among many, unique but also normal, in the familiar nationalist mold" (Slezkine 268). Of course, as with the founders, the youth movements that developed after 1920 were involved in ideological disputes despite Katznelson's plea for unity. However, when there were defectors, they were despised, but free to go. As one student of the Herziliya Gymnasium wrote in 1937,"this is the nation that has produced great heroes, zealous for freedom and from whom have arose prophets who prophesied the rule of justice and honesty in the world" (Slezkine 268).

In the struggle for the unity of the Democratic-Socialist society, Berl Katznelson and Yitzchak Tabenkin clashed not because they were anti-socialist or anti-communalism, but because they viewed the development of the Settlement Society in different ways. Their ability to debate and later compromise on their differences is displayed in the December 1919 conference that led to the establishment of the General Federation of Labor (Histadrut) the next year. This ability to compromise on their vision of collectivism and communalism in Palestine would have a major impact on the modern State of Israel after 1948.

# II

## HISTORICAL BACKGROUND OF THE FIRST AND SECOND ALIYOT

*La Hachshara, La Aliyah, La Kibbutz, La Haganah (To the Training Farm, To Immigrate, To the Kibbutz, To The Defense Force).*

In the late Nineteenth Century, "although the tsarist regime discriminated against the Jews and severely restricted their rights of residence, it did not always interfere too deeply in the religious and cultural affairs of the Jewish community" (Frank, Ben 64). Many Jewish organizations enjoyed a national and religious semi-autonomy within the framework of the Jewish Community Council. Thus, the Jewish community did develop a meaningful Jewish life and culture in spite of the discrimination and persecution. (Frank, Ben 64)

In terms of the education in Europe that the young Jewish intellectuals of the late Nineteenth and early Twentieth Centuries received, one can survey the leadership of *Ha-poel ha-Tzair* and *Poale Zion* and note that all of them knew Yiddish and Hebrew and studied Jewish literature, unlike the Bolsheviks who could not put out a Yiddish or Hebrew paper after the Winter Palace fell to them in 1917 (Frank, Ben 120). In general, the Socialist-Zionists had a strong background in Jewish culture. Amongst those leaders were Berl Katznelson, Ben Gurion, Nachman Syrkin, Dov Ber Borochov, Yitzchak Tabenkin, Manya Shohat, Joseph Brenner, and Aleph Dalet Gordon.

In the late nineteenth century, the Heder Metukan was established. It was the reform or reconstructed *heder*, a religious school in which there was daily attendance and which was a manifestation of the changes introduced in Eastern Europe by the National Awakening Movement in its effort to create "the new Jew." Its relevance for the young intelligentsia studying Hebrew was extremely limited. Reformers considered neither the Haskalah enlightenment, Jewish education, nor the *hederim* adequate to their ideals.

The major reformers were Haim Nachman Bialik, the famous Zionist National Awakening Poet who wrote about the tragic Pogrom in Kishinev in 1903 and the Jewish plight in Eastern Europe as well as the Histadrut workers' anthem, Techhazakna; and the well-known organizer of new *hederim*, Menachem Mendel Ussishkin. As early as 1868-1884, Hebrew socialists formed around the periodical *Ha Shahar* (The Dawn). Among the Hebrew socialists affiliated with *Ha-Shahar* was Aaron Lieberman, who "sought to conduct socialist propaganda in Hebrew among the Jews in the Pale." Neither Lieberman, nor most Hebrew socialists linked to *Ha-Shachar* were Zionists, since the original goal of this organization was to create a secular Hebrew language culture; but the outbreak of pogroms in 1881 (after the Czar Alexander was assassinated) had the effect of turning many if not most Hebraists into Zionists (Wolfe, Robert 219-220).

The First Aliyah settlers from Eastern Europe landed in Jaffa and immediately settled on land (actually in a hotel) purchased by Moroccan Jews who had made Aliyah in the 1840s (Eliach 171-172). At that time, there were also neighborhoods such as Neve Tzedek in what would later become South Tel Aviv. For hundreds of years, there had been neighborhoods in Jaffa, Tiberias, Safed, Hebron, and Jerusalem.

By 1884, the Lovers of Zion (*Hovevei Zion*) was established and organized a fund for Jewish immigration to Palestine. Centered in Odessa, the Lovers of Zion was composed mainly of Russian Jews. In Odessa, there were cultural Zionists as well. Odessa was a cosmopolitan city in which other well-known cultural Zionists, and Jewish secular writers lived, a few such as Isaac Babel supported the Communist regime. They included many prominent writers and men who were and became ideological and political leaders in Europe and in Palestine: Issac Babel, Haim Nachman Bialik, Leon Pinsker, Menachem Mendel Ussishkin, Moses Lieb Lilienblum, Meir Dizengoff, David Frishman, Mendel Mokher Seforim, and Ahad Ha-Am (Frank, Ben 376-379).

The most famous of these people was Ahad Ha Am, meaning 'one of the people' (His real name was Asher Ginzburg). He was the central figure in the Hebraist movement he was not a socialist. In fact, his conflicts with "official Zionism" was more on one or another of the phases of the Zionist program than on the movement as a whole. He was one who was more interested in the spread of Hebrew and Jewish secular culture in Europe, America, and the

Diaspora in general, and that the Jewish community would be construed as the vanguard community of Western standing outside the politics of the West. He promulgated a fixed and independent center for national culture, for learning, art, and literature." (Goettheil 192, 229). His major goal was that Palestine would become the worldwide spiritual center for the Jewish people. He was a critic of the manner in which colonization was then attempted (by the First Aliyah), even though he was a leader of the earlier *Hovevei Zion* enthusiasm. Asher Ginzburg was described once as a Zionist who was more interested in the souls of the settlers than in the settlements (Wolfe, Robert 221).

The location of the societies which prepared for aliyah to *Eretz Israel* while also propagating Zionist and Socialist ideology existed mostly in the Pale: the Ukraine, Poland, and White Russia, but even in Rumania by the end of 1881, there were thirty settlement societies. In Lithuania, from where David Wolfson the second President of the Zionist Movement came, his teacher was a major participant in *Hovevei Zion*. In fact, on January 11th and 12[th,] a conference was held in Focsani, Rumania that set up a headquarters for *Hovevei Zion* in Galati. Later, after the Kishinev and Gomel Pogroms in 1903, the societies in Russia which had been in existence since the turn of the Century received calls from Josef Vitkin and M. Ussishkin, in the latter's pamphlet, "Our Program", to make aliyah and to set up agricultural settlements. Those calls were later heard by the settlers of the Second Aliyah such as as David Ben Gurion, Berl Katznelson, Itzchak Ben-Zvi, Joseph Sprinzak, and others.

A large percentage of the Russian Jews who would immigrate in the First Aliyah had a relationship to the Zerubavel society set up in Odessa in 1883 with Leon Pinsker as chairman and Moses Leib Lilenblum as secretary. The Odessa Committee retained a major influence in *Hovevei Zion's* preparation of the first immigrants to Israel in our modern era. One of Ben Gurion's essays in *Rebirth and Destiny* gives Pinsker credit for being an ideological comrade of Socialist-Zionists. He quotes his speech at Katowicz at the first Conference of Hovevei Zion.

"The frightful condition of Jewry will not change for the better unless we succeed in finding it a new place to live in, and a new kind of life; unless we pave a new way for it, a way based on skills and on handiwork. Every nation lives on its soil. And among the sons of most nations many farmers: their well-being flows from the sweat of their brow and the reward of their labors is solid and can be seen and grasped which bear fruit in the every day meaning of the word. We must gather up what is left of our vigor and trek to the open spaces..." (Ben Gurion 45-46).

Despite its excellent work, however, in assisting colonization and furthering the dissemination of culture among the Jews of Palestine; and despite the fact that it helped Jews come to the realization that Eretz Israel was the most suitable territory for the Jewish state, some authors of that time, such as Richard Gottheil, claimed that it failed to utilize the rare opportunity it had of making its program large, bold, and statesmanlike. However, the Zeruvabel society did become the central society of Hovevei Zion, and thus with it leading the way, the First Aliyah was put into motion. Many of Hovevei Zion leadership had earlier put their hopes in Alliance Israelite Universelle and other organizations for funds, but those organizations sought haven for Jewish refugees who were concentrated in places such as Brody, Poland, not in Palestine, but in the United States, or even in other places in Russia. In a unified way, all the Jewish societies which had decided to make aliyah from 1881 on agreed that they had to create a class of farmers and artisans. The key agreement between the supporting philanthropic societies and the settlers, was that they were both practical Zionists and believed that the major task of Zionism was the settlement of the Jews on the land in Palestine (Gottheil 72-73).

Finally, another different type of major supporter of Hovevei Zion and the First Aliyah, who was not a Socialist, was Rabbi Smuel Mohilever. He was an Orthodox Jew who did believe in the movement's chance to succeed. He had joined the Hovevei Zion in the late 1870s and was also a founder of the Odessa Committee. A rabbi, who was the head of a Yeshiva in Bialostok, he knew that there was a time for action, and he gave his soul to Hovevei Zion. He is credited with going to Baron De Rothschild in Paris and convincing him to set up orchards in Rishon le Zion. Mohilever understood that the masses must be convinced to make Aliyah not with Biblical phrases but concrete and logical suggestions. He thus became one of the most prominent Orthodox leaders in Hovevei Zion and in the Orthodox Zionist movement, Mizrachi. He knew that the movement had not been nourished by irreligious sources. He was one of the Odessa committee leaders who, animated by a strong national sentiment, and he was one of a few prominent Orthodox people who set great store in the first modest attempts to colonize Palestine.

Other than Rabbi Mohilever, the leaders of the *Hovevei* movement included Moses Lev Lilienblum, Peretz Smolenski, Professor Shapira of Heidelberg, Professor Mandelstamm of Kiev and Leo Levanda. By 1881, the leadership advocated settling in *Eretz Israel*, and there were journals supporting that idea. These included Ha-Shahar, Ha-Maggid, Ha Meliz, and Razsvet (Russian), all organs of the *Hovevei Zion* movement. *Hovevei's* student society, founded in 1881 in Saint Petersburg, declared that "every son of Israel that admits that there is no salvation for Israel unless they establish a government of their own in the land of Israel can be a member of the society." Almost every Jew except the richest ones in Russia advocated for settlement in Israel (*Zionism* 13-14).

At the Berlin Conference in 1882, most of the Jewish organizations opposed settling refugees in *Eretz Israel*. However, *Hovevei Zion's* representatives who backed the proposal of Israel Hildesheimer (a famous German Rabbinical scholar) sent over settler groups and that angered the Turks and motivated them to publish orders closing the entry into Palestine by immigrants. *Hovevei Zion* immediately called on its British sympathizer Laurence Oliphant, a British Christian Zionist who later settled in Haifa, but he lacked the influence to move the Turks away from their position.

Nevertheless, in 1882 the only group of pioneers, sixteen young Russian Jews who planned to settle on the land, made their way to Palestine. They did so without ensuring property to work on as agricultural workers, arriving in Jaffa on July 11. In that month, Zalman Levontin and his friends established Rishon le-Zion, one of the earliest pioneers of the First Aliyah (Near 8). The pioneers never intended to populate the cities that already existed. The settlements during the first aliyot were always agricultural. These sixteen were the first wave of a tiny group that never numbered more than 525, in settling what is now the fourth largest city in Israel. This first movement called itself BILU, after the initials Beit Ya'akov lechu v'nelcha—"house of Jacob, come go and be going." The phrase was taken from the Prophet Isaiah and was adopted by the small group of students form Kharkov in the Ukraine. "Their aim was to rebuild the ancient Jewish homeland on principles of social justice and self-labor" (in Builders and Dreamers, Editors J.J.Goldberg and Elliot King, Herzl Press New York, 1993, The essay, "The Early Years" by Moshe Cohen, 31).

Although the BILU were the impetus for the First Aliyah pioneers who followed, they had not reckoned with a number of obstacles-hostile Turkish officialdom; an old Jewish population steeped in medieval ways and suspicious of the "revolutionary" spirit of the newcomers; a large reservoir of unorganized, exploited Arab workers to whom independence and modern standards were unknown; a difficult climate; and a stubborn neglected soil that was slow to yield before hands so long divorced from hard physical labor; they still did begin the long trek toward new social and economic horizons for their people (Kurland 6).

Shortly after that, settlers from the Moinesti society of Rumania reached Rosh Pina (originally settled by people from Safed but abandoned), while at the same time, Petach Tikvah, near Tel Aviv, which originally had been settled by families from Jerusalem but abandoned, was also resettled. Kfar Saba (today another suburban area of Tel Aviv) was added to the list of villages. From 1878-1894, a total of 28 agricultural villages ranging in size from a handful in Kfar Saba to 800 in Petach Tikvah and Zichron Yaakov (south of Haifa, on the coast) were founded and began the initial economic development stage. In those first sixteen years, a total of 5,700 arrived out of a total of 50,000 Jews in the country

Some Jewish Eastern Europeans arrived as if they were making a pilgrimage, such as those traditional ones that had occurred throughout the history of the Exile, while others came as an inspiration to Jews world wide and as refuge in time of need. Between 1880 (the official First Aliyah date) and 1905 when the Second Aliyah began, there were 25,000 immigrants from Russia to Palestine. In comparison, the mass immigration of that period enlarged the Jewish community in America from 280,000 in 1880 to one million in 1900. (Near, 7-11; and for a more detailed account of the numbers of settlers and settlements, see Walter Laqueur, A History of Zionism; Eliav and Rosenthal's First Aliyah Chapters 3 and 4).

Rumanians supported by *Hovevei Zion* reached Zichron Yaakov (then called Zammarin), but the meager resources of all the new pioneering settlers caused them to ask for help from the societies in Russia and Rumania. Unable to provide needed assistance, Samuel Fineberg (of Rishon le-Zion which was south of Tel Aviv) and Rabbi Mohliever turned to Baron Edmond de Rothschild to help a group of settlers from Russia settle in Israel (Later they settled in Ekron), and to take Rishon le–Zion under his protection. Thus the private business support of the Baron became the watchword of the First Aliyah, and that colony and a later one at Zichron Yaakov established the non-collective private agricultural enterprise (Zionism 15-16).

In all, the Baron's colonies including Zichron Yaakov, Yesod ha-Ma'ala, Metullah, in the northern Galilee, Petach Tikvah, Ekron, Rishon le–Zion, and Rosh Pinah cost the Baron a large sum of money for the founding and their upkeep. Various estimates have it to be over forty-sixty million francs and even up to sixty million francs from 1882-1900 (Kurland 10; Weisgal 201-203).

Although it was hard for him to disengage from responsibility that this expenditure carried with it, he did so in 1899. He handed over whatever interest he still had in the colonies to the Jewish Colonization Societies (Gottheil 80-81). Eventually middle class Jewish colonists controlled the farms in Judea, Samaria and the Galilee. In that these were private agricultural enterprises, the Second Aliyah socialists were to have strained relationships with them (Shapira 24-25).

In hindsight, we know that there was not a Zionist Movement to help the settlers financially or offer assistance in the difficult period of economic development after the land was purchased. The settlers had to purchase the wide areas of cultivable land from absentee owners. They accomplished that task despite the government of the Ottoman Empire actively preventing Western peoples from establishing perceived footholds in the country. For instance, Jews were forbidden the purchase of land, and to circumvent Turkish practices, the settlers used bribery and ruses.

Also an issue was the lack of security. The Ottoman Empire did not establish strong governmental rule in Palestine, meaning that law and order in Palestine was lax and security became an issue when Bedouin tribes from Jordan made regular incursions.

After seeing that it was brigands which forced the original farmers to sell, albeit at high prices, the Jewish agriculturalists retreated to more hilly areas, difficult of access and near their homes, and thus more easily defensible (Near 8-9). The only other group besides *Hovevei Zion* which encouraged the settlers from Eastern Europe was the J.C.A. itself (Jewish Colonization Association) "whose Palestinian operation was only part of a world-wide scheme to encourage Jews to engage in agriculture." However, the J.C.A. did not (actually) help the 'worker-settler.' The non-socialist administrators tried in every way to put down manifestations of the autonomy on the part of the workers; in order to keep the settlers under close control, they tried to get them to sign declarations that they were only hired workers and not permanent settlers.

For a long time, the Biluim (plural of the workers of the early BILU movement) who settled in Gedera refused to submit to the yoke of the J.C.A's administration, but were unable to carry out their mission, either. There was no intrinsic justification of their existence in as much as the workers became settlers, and the early organizations lacked order and the basic principles of a workers movement. The cause of their collapse was their ideological confusion, since they were content to allow the actual labor on their members' farms to be done partly by non-Jewish hired workers who were often seasonal, since the cash crops were grapes and citrus fruits (Arabs from the neighborhood of the moshava or in some cases Arabs who lived in the moshava were the hired workers-so much part of the scene had they become).

The men worked in the fields and the Arab women were domestic servants. The other problem was that the policy of the J.C.A. centered on redeeming land and men by capital alone (Preuss 20-21; Near 15). It soon became apparent that to empower Zionism, a new path would have to be beaten; new blood would have to be introduced into the land. Joseph Vitkin issued the call to the Jewish youth of the Diaspora to come to Palestine as "embittered heroes who will fight for their ideals like desperate ones without the slightest thought of retreat" (Kurland 10).

They did come in answer to Vitkin's call. They came ready for a struggle. They had a deep consciousness of the social and economic implications of that struggle for themselves and for their people. They followed Vitkin's view that stated that you do not have to wait for the end of the world in order to achieve *ge'ula*-salvation, but you could reach it by *tikun atzmi*, self-improvement-starting with oneself and doing what one could.

# III

## THE SECOND ALIYAH, & THE SETTLEMENT MOVEMENT, 1905-1919

*"Oh who can save us hunger's dread?*
*Who always gave us ample bread,*
*And milk to drink when we are fed?*
*"Whom shall we praise, whom shall we bless?*
*To work and toil our thankfulness."*
*Hiiyam Nachman Bialik*
*"The Song of Work and Toil"*
*—from Builders and Dreamers*

Although critical of the first Aliyah and its weaknesses, including the acceptance of management hiring Arab leader, its failed social experiments and its inability to create small, self-sufficient groups within a national labor movement, the pioneers of the Second Aliyah in time were forced to confront the same challenges as their forebearers, and suffered their own disillusionment, challenges, and confrontations between collectivist idealism and the realities of living in Palestine.

From 1904-1914 the population of Palestinian Jews rose to 50,000 while into the USA poured 850,000 Jewish immigrants in the same decade. It is estimated by 1914 that there were only 2,500 Jewish workers in Palestine. Joseph Brenner wrote that, "Sevenfold more depart than arrive…Palestine regrettably is a tourist country for our brethren as well. They come, they see… and they return…" (Shapira 25 quoting from "Between the Waters" in Joseph

Brenner's Collected Works). By the time of the First Histadrut Conference in December 1920, there were only 4,333 workers (Kurland 21).

The estimates of the percentage that remained in Palestine after only one decade range from Ben Gurion's estimate of ten percent remaining to sixty-seven percent staying. Although there was much criticism of the First Aliyah, the Second Aliyah used some of the First Aliyah cooperative ideas and experiments which they adapted ex-post facto to add historical depth and continuity to the kibbutz movement (Kurland 11).

The Second Aliyah elite was definitely the successors of the First Aliyah. The people of the Second Aliyah at first settled in the existing moshavot. Almost all of them were young. For example the founders of Degania, the first kibbutz, averaged seventeen years old. Although the statistics are difficult to find, the majority were unmarried, and the vast majority were male, probably never more than 20 percent ever were female during the Second Aliyah. In the Third Aliyah, we know that more than 70 percent were male (Near 15-16). The women who had to live in towns toward the end of the Second Aliyah (after 1918) were depressed in the towns, since they were homemakers according to the British style of the day if married, and usually out of work if single.

At first, they were even unhappy in the *kvutzot*, since their roles were limited to work in the children's houses, the laundry rooms, the sewing rooms and cooking. They were hardly ever allowed to toil in the fields. They never were considered equal in terms of work opportunities and lost the dignity of the 'conquest of labor', seldom being material-producing laborers. This was especially evident in the first collectives, since the women who were forced to work in the kitchen had the food they cooked at times returned in lines of trays by the men of their *kvutza* or kibbutz.

It is important to understand that these men and women were both from diverse ideological Jewish Socialist backgrounds and influenced by Russian revolutionary groups. By 1915, certain women in the settlements were becoming part of the revolutionary leadership, including Manya Shohat, Rachel Yanait, and Miriam Baratz who created their own Women's Workers Movement. The spirit of the 1905 Revolution had reached them, even after the disillusioning failure to create a democratic Russia and satisfy their goal of developing a 'New Man' and 'New Woman'. This notwithstanding, these women still promoted a greater equality than Western women would otherwise see for at least fifty years.

The majority of the Second Aliyah radicals believed that the moral, political, and cultural evils which resulted from the economic structure of the Jewish people could be cured only by creating a Jewish working class. Since this could only be brought about one way, the young pioneers of 1904, previously divorced from productive labor, became workers. In Palestine, this translated mainly into becoming agricultural workers.

Following the examples of A. D. Gordon, Joseph Brenner, Manya Shohat, Rachel Yanait, Berl Katznelson, and Ben Gurion, all of who made Aliyah between 1904 and 1911, the pioneers stressed conquering themselves for labor. "...to persevere despite the objective difficulties and by changing his/her nature to bring about 'salvation' for himself and the Jewish people" (Near 17).

In order to achieve their goals of conquering labor and establishing self-sufficient farms, the workers received some help from the J.C.A. and from the Jewish National Fund. The J.N.F. acquired a charter in 1903, and in 1907-1908 began to provide the land and expertise to the workers. After World War I, the leaders of the Zionist movement had seen the establishment of the expanded Jewish Agency as one way of relieving the economic distress in the recession of the mid 1920's. By that time, the process of settlement had taken on completely regular administrative form. The land had been acquired by the Jewish National Fund and allocated by its directorate to settlement groups according to priorities established through consultation with the appropriate organ of the Histadrut ha-Klalit (established in 1920). Start up capital, livestock, and initial loans for equipment were provided by the Keren ha-Yesod (Palestine Foundation Fund). That body became responsible for the financial stability of the settlements until they were able to function independently (Near 171).

During the early years of the Second Aliyah, some of the leaders who were workers as well as Manya Shohat and members of Bar Giora, a secretly-organized guard group, were already using their own strategies to advance the social experiments which during the First Aliyah had failed. By 1909, the Jewish National Fund Company called the Land of Israel Department also existed in Jaffa. Its task was solely to help Jewish farmers settle on the land. In 1907, the Zionist movement had finally moved to settlement activities by sending Arthur Ruppin to Palestine where he would set up training farms on land purchased by the J.N.F. By 1918, the Jewish National Fund controlled 223,000 dunam, which it could lease. The first successful experiment was created after a strike at Kineret. It took place on a small portion of that farm land which had been the Arab village of Um Juni (Near 18;24).

Although the workers and Arthur Ruppin did not use the same method as Manya Shohat and members of the defense group Bar Giora organized in their collective at Sejera, (Self–sufficient labor was created in Sejera with the agreement of the manager Eliyahu Krauzen who allowed the workers to use the animals and farm tools and divide the profit with management at the end of the year), Ruppin's experiment which was at first kept a secret so that the Zionist movement would not react negatively for funding the project if it failed, also arose out of a strategy developed by him and the workers' political and agricultural organizations of the Galilee. This cooperation which occurred between the Ha-Poel ha-Tzair workers and the Jewish National Fund created the successful model of the kvutza (This model at first never had more than twelve members in it) in Palestine. By 1909, there were five working kvuzot and four self-defense group including over seventy men and women (Labor Zionist Handbook; Near 26).

The kvutzot (plural for kvutza) included Kineret and Merchavia, the latter which had workers and members of the Watchmen (ha-Shomer), a small group of men and women who had to fight incursions into the fields and plough them at the same time in order to confirm their right to settle the land. They were joined by a permanent group of settlers chosen by a J.C.A. manager who helped train them in Galacia and who actually joined them in Merchavia. Merchavia went through three stages: first the expert agriculturalists came; workers were then added; and lastly the workers had a choice to be separate or collectivists. This occurred at the same time that the Hadera group (ex-Kineret strikers) finally joined the Um Juni kvutza (Near 31). The term Hachshara (agricultural training) was thus made famous. Later in the Diaspora as well in Palestine itself, a catchy melody for La Hachshara, La Aliyah, La Kibbutz, La Haganah made its way through the youth movements (to the Training, to Immigrate to Israel, To Kibbutz, To Defense). By 1914, Merchavia itself, after much experimentation, became a kvutza on the model of the successful Degania (Near 36).

Following a strike by workers fed up with the hiring of cheap Arab labor by the foreman Moshe Berman in 1909, Ruppin, as a sop to the striking farm workers, suggested they form a 'conquest group' and move to JNF land at Um Juni, a relatively isolated piece of land on the Kineret farm. Although they were forced to leave Kineret, they refused to accept Ruppin's offer. However, the concept of collective production by a small group of workers living together attracted the attention of other workers of the Settlement Society, and six members including two women were picked by the Galilee organizations and parties to go to Um Juni. Katznelson joined them after hearing about their collective experiment. This young ideological leader of the future referred to his experience as one where a young inexperienced worker suffering from malaria was honored to be allowed to join their "work-work than which I have never seen any more serious or more pure." As at Sejera, they ended the year with a small profit (Shapira 44-47; Near 26-27).

Meanwhile the commune at Hadera, where the land was also bought by the Jewish National Fund, and which was settled in 1909 by the strikers from Kineret, evolved into its own commune. The Hadera commune consisted of workers who worked for different farmers but pooled their earnings and ate meals together. Eventually, Ruppin convinced them to join the group at Um Juni that under the leadership of Joseph Bussel, they did in 1910. By that time, this group of mainly Ha Poel ha-Tzair followers who followed their spiritual mentor A.D. Gordon now displayed confidence that "a Jewish farmer could make a living in Palestine from his own labor" (Near 30-31).

Um Juni, which later was called Degania, was the model *kvutza*, and in it, as in most of the other *kvutzot* after 1910 were communal consumption and communal production. Even in ha-Shomer groups, where at times a wife cooked for her husband who was guarding, there were variations; for example, one woman cooked for a group of guards (Near 31). By 1914, the Degania model had become the established standard model of the kvutzot.

Later, Degania was in conflict with the labor institution Hamashbir (1916) because it wished the kvutza to succeed more so then serve the entire workers' society. It occurred because the concept of Hamashbir (Crisis) was to operate on the assumption that each settlement would sell its crops to the labor institution for a low price at the beginning of the season, and thus Hamashbir could sell it to the workers at cost. This concept and the plan arose because the Turks were confiscating crops during World War I and scarcity and speculation caused a steep rise in the prices. In Degania, one leader stated that the kvutza should sell its crops on the open market for a better price. Kineret had been the first kvutza to accept the concept of workers' society survival over the individual kvutza; and a delegation was therefore sent from Kineret to Degania. Eventually, Degania with much prodding by Berl Katznelson, Meir Rutberg, A.D. Gordon, and others agreed to place the general good over its own interests (Shapira 64).

By 1911/1912, there were three different types of contractual groups: defense groups of ha-Shomer; working groups such as Degania (as Um Juni was known after 1911); and settlement groups of which only one Merchavia was known at that stage. From then until the establishment of the State of Israel, both of the latter settlement groups (*kvutzot hityashvut*) and working groups (*kvutzot avodah*) continued to exist side by side, although both the relationship between them and the terminology changed. (In 1919, the defense groups ceased to exist when ha-Shomer was disbanded). From that time, the term *kvutza* came to have the generic connotation of a communal group which was organized for a purpose and limited in time, and thus it retained that meaning until the end of the Second Aliyah and the introduction of the word 'kibbutz' in 1920 (beginning of the Third Aliyah period).

As for the historical beginnings of Degania, Joseph Baratz wrote in his famous book, Village By The Jordan, that conditions were miserable when they first arrived. "The air buzzed with mosquitoes and it lay heavy and close between the hills. The flat valley was like a hot plate, the heat pressed on it. Everything was burnt brown. The river was a trickle. But when the rain came, it flooded the land and when the waters withdrew they left swamps and mud" (Baratz 49-50).

To get to the fields and houses they had to bring up the mud with pails on barrels. They even had to use mules-two big tins to each mule, then barrels on the carts. For two months, they were surrounded by mud. They had to spend years fighting down the malaria. They planted eucalyptus trees to drain the swamps, and as more fields came under cultivation, it helped to drain the swamps. Then the Rutenberg canalization scheme was used to channel the water into canals and use it for irrigation, leaving the rest of the land drained. Finally they had an anti-malarial gang put down DDT wherever the mosquitoes bred.

Of the twelve people who arrived with Baratz, ten were men and two were women. The reason for this number was that six men were to plow, two to act as watchmen, one as a secretary-accountant, and one in reserve. The two women were to do the housekeeping. Later in the summer, robbers used a ford to cross the Jordan River, and the twelve inhabitants of Um Juni realized two watchmen were not enough. From that time on, they took turns standing guard (just as occurs in the kibbutzim of today where guard duty is done by rotation) (Baratz 50-51).

In the beginning, they had only grain crops. They tilled the soil with primitive tools, without farm animals except for the six pair of mules and two horses. The Palestine Office supplied the farmers with the plows and the seed. There was a contract with the Palestine Office; and the accountant Joseph Bussel had to be in contact regularly with Dr Ruppin who Baratz and his comrades said was a good friend. In any case, they reported to him everything they did and he gave them good advice and—"comforted them in their troubles and rejoiced when things went well." It was clear from Baratz's writing that he left them in complete charge (Baratz 52-53).

One of the major problems in the *kvutzot* and even in the early days of the *kibbutzim* of the Second Aliyah was the issue of womens' work. Baratz admitted that all the men in the *kvutza* worked happily, but the women at first were not happy. The reason why there were only two he admitted was because the men thought that women could only cook and wash. The women wanted the experience of farming and were certainly jealous. Besides the mental hardship, the physical conditions under which the women worked were not satisfying. There were neither stoves, nor kerosene, not to speak of electricity.

One day the women came to them and complained, and even then the men could not understand how their mothers had been happy cooking and the two women were not. Finally, after the women refused to give them any rest for weeks, the men gave in, and they bought cows and chickens and began even to grow vegetables, so that there could be work for the women. However, every time a new branch of agriculture was opened, the question arose should a man or woman work in that branch?

Although Degania changed over time in that respect, and many women did work in agriculture there and elsewhere by the end of World War I (Sarah Malkin and Tehia Leiberman for example insisted on doing so until they succeeded), this issue continued to plague many other *kvutzot* and *kibbutzim*. Women never did quite reach the expectations of equality or the 'conquest of labor' in the *kvutzot* or in the *kibbutzim* (Baratz 54-5; Near 49; 86).

The other issues which involved the women were marriage and the children's houses. After Baratz returned from the army in Russia, serving well for three months and then stealing out of camp and getting on a boat back to Palestine, (He and his wife to be Miriam had returned so he could serve, and his parents would not have to pay the 500 rubles fine. Baratz as many other pioneers in Israel was not then a legal resident in Palestine), he and others in Um Juni built the permanent settlement of Degania. Although the original group had made an agreement while still at Um Juni not to marry for five years, one young member married a girl who had arrived from Russia and with whom he had fallen in love with in three weeks. This was the second wedding that occurred after moving into the permanent settlement. Joseph Baratz's and Miriam's, the first Degania wedding, was manifested by a large and joyous celebration. Thd wedding was attended by Turks and Arabs from Tiberias and even people from Jaffe two days away, besides the hundreds of Jewish chaluzim from the Galilee. The young couple whose wedding was the second one had a third child years later. His name was Moshe Dayan (Baratz 58-59; 62).

The children's houses for which the *kibbutzim* are so famous and about which controversy was recalled later were instituted in the first *kvutzot*. Baratz mentions their existence in Degania when Miriam, Joseph Baratz's wife, had two children and took them everywhere she went. She even traveled with them in to Ben Shemen to a special seminar in agriculture. The *kvutza* soon realized that all women were not as strong as she was, and decided the children's upbringing and the education was the responsibility of the entire community. They chose one young woman soon after that to be the 'house mother'. As Degania changed in that regard, other developments created the chance for women to work in agriculture. The main one was the training of women in agricultural work at the training farm at Sejera and then first and then in the agricultural training school in Kineret. By the end of World War I, all women including mothers officially had the right to work in agriculture (Baratz 72-73; Near 87).

Women's work and the growth of the *kvutzot* not only forced the kvutzot to face issues of equality, whereby kitchen workers were to receive the same rewards as field workers but also the basic issue of democratic governance. It was reported that in Degania informal discussions were held every evening about work details for the next day. During the pre-World War I period of 1913-1914 these meetings could last all night. Once in 1916, a customary general meeting general meeting concerning the state of the kvutza, the plan for the following year, or dealing with a special problem, actually started Friday and lasted until Saturday evening. This led to the custom of one discussion a week on Saturday night that persists in most *kibbutzim* to this day (Near 37-38).

With regard to sexual equality, two aspects are distinct. Women had unquestioned rights within the discussions of the *kvutza*. They took part in all the general meetings and could speak and vote as exactly as did the men. Near the end of his life, the founding leader of Degania Joseph Bussel proudly proclaimed that economic equality was the crowning achievement of the *kvutza* (Near 86).

By 1917, Degania consisted of forty members, yet its soverign governing body was still the general meeting. However, soon there was seasonal work to do and hired labor to use, and the work schedule became more complicated even as it grappled over the use of that hired labor. Before 1917, few women had actually worked in agriculture. This changed by the end of the Second Aliyah. The growth in population and complexity of work in the formerly small *kvutzot* led to a four man work committee which decided on work assignments and other things as well. This led to resentment between the new comers and the veterans. Some of the kvutzot as Degania even considered returning to a ten men and two women membership limit during World War I, but made other choices–not to expand as did Kineret, but to find work for its members outside the kvutza and improve its society and economy.

Before the end of World War I, in all of the first kvutzot, there were eventually 'house mothers', but in the relationship between the kvutza and the Zionist Movement there was no mention of women in the contracts. The women received their economic support separately from the Zionist settlement department. Thus, early on, economically and socially, their positions had been weak. As mentioned, Sarah Malkin was one woman who never accepted this arrangement, and at one point she left Degania when they did not allow her to work in agriculture. She returned many years later (Near 44-49).

In *Israel: A Spiritual Travel Guide*, Hoffman (Jewish Light Publishing, Woodstock Vermont, 1998), quotes Manya Shohat's daughter as saying that the children lived in two houses, sleeping six to seven in a room and sometimes four in a bed. She also stated that she felt like an orphan and that when other children went at 4:00 to be with their parents she had nowhere to go. Although she never gave it serious thought, she wrote that she did pity herself. Mixed up with the feeling of not being good enough was the concept of the Homeland. She then added the finishing touch by telling a story that when Ben Gurion once asked her something about her parents, she told him that she was an orphan, not knowing how those words escaped her. He got angry and told her that she should not dare to speak like that of her parents again, that because of her parents the settlement existed (Hoffman 91-92).

In Ludwig Lewisohn's book *Israel*, he explicitly mentions seeing the children's houses; and the parents snatching what seemed to him a pitiful and crowded glimpse of both the children and each other before the dinner hour being over, each had to return to his or her appointed task. (Lewisohn 179-180).

This type of alienation of parents, especially mothers and daughters, was a problem which has come to light in our times, since the children's upbringing was hardly ever the parents' responsibility and had an averse affect on many veteran mothers and children of *kvutzot* or *kibbutzim*. However, the collective raising of children did create the well-known peer group education and led to the effective leadership roles of kibbutz youth in the *Haganah* (Defense Force) and the I.D.F. (Israel Defense Forces) before and after the State was established.

Ein Harod was a *kvutza* of the *Gedud ha-Avodah* during World War I, which helped settle the hundreds of refugees turned away from Jaffa by Turks fearing a British invasion in 1917 (Near 45). This presented many *kvutzot* with a solution in in the waning days of the Second Aliyah. The *Gedud ha-Avodah* was prominent especially during the British Mandate in developing the 'conquest of labor' and the self-sufficiency of the *kvutzot* and *kibbutzim* from 1917-1924(The official end of the Third Aliyah) Thus, the 'Building of the Roads' Period which was the major method of employing hundreds of kvutza or kibbutz members, the majority who were followers of A.D. Gordon, solved many issues of employment, and other pressing issues. It also created a practical need that led to the institutionalization of the children's houses. Its ability to absorb workers toward the end of the Second Aliyah was a major factor in that Wave's success.

Although Degania was a model *kvutza*, it was not guarded as were the ha-Shomer *kvutzot*. Its members did not see themselves as being responsible for the Settlement Society's security until harvest-time Bedouin incursions killed three members of the Lower Galilee *kvutzot*.

The housing was much better in Degania than in Um Juni, and the food supply was adequate, but mostly vegetarian with occasionally fish when it could be obtained. Although the majority of the new houses were well built when the numbers began to grow, some men had to move into tents.

Culturally life there was rudimentary. In many kvutzot and kibbutzim, there was a certain anti-intellectual element because the total focus was on dedication to work. However, there were many avid readers and the tone was cultured and tolerant. During the first two years of Degania's existence, Yiddish was spoken but after the arrival of a Hebrew teacher in 1913, only Hebrew was spoken in accordance with the ideology (Near 39). There were no religious institutions such as synagogues or rabbis in the kvutzot, nor in the kibbuzim during any of the first three aliyot.

In the first years, the major crops of Degania were arable—half wheat and the rest divided between oats, sorghum, and various legumes. The workers used European models of farm equipment adapted to local conditions. Help toward successful harvests arrived in the form of mechanization with the introduction of the threshing machine in 1914. Experimental orchards were planted which included fruit, olives, and almonds, but during the first years they were too young to yield any fruit. Vegetables such as cucumbers, carrots, and radishes were grown for home consumption. Dairy and poultry livestock were also considered part of the home garden. By the last pre-war year, after suffering a cattle plague that hindered the economic progress, Degania had reached comparative prosperity (Near 39-40).

Berl Katznelson, as many of the young members of the Second Aliyah, lived and worked in many settlements. One day, he was in Petach Tikvah and the next day his mood induced him to leave and go to Hadera. This gypsy-like quality and this need not to be attached to one place or job, even to a particular person was a characteristic inherent in the history of the Second Aliyah. The ha-Shomer watchmen dreamed of expanding horizons and living on frontiers. They dressed with swirling kefiyot as they rode their horses, enamored by the Palestinian Arab peasants whose labor market they were forced to share at first.

Katznelson himself worked in Ein Ganim, Hadera, Sejera, Um Juni, and again in Ein Ganim. All such journeys were conducted on foot. "Free of their elders and the stifling authority and conventional restraints, their clothes were shabby and the food meager." Despite problems, Berl felt free as a bird: I have cast off the whole world...(Shapira 35).

However, the problem of illness followed him and many hundreds of others in the Second Aliyah. For example, he arrived at Hadera where malaria had killed many, driving both settlers and laborers from the colony. At Kineret, when Ruppin asked the manager where the lavatory was, the farm manager Berman said the whole world is yours. He absolutely refused to put up such a modern installation in a rural area. The pioneers in that kvutza lived among the dirt and mud, and healthy and ill lay side by side. "The appalling living conditions, together with the unsanitary food and the exhausting physical labor, promoted disease" (Shapira 43).

There were no nurses at the farm and medical supplies were confined to a tin box of quinine powder, which stood on the dining table and which workers sprinkled over their food. One worker fell ill with yellow fever and was transferred to the hospital in Tiberius where he died a few days later. Conditions there had already becoming unbearable and the workers had organized one half of a day strike with four demands. They told Berman that he needed to repair the living conditions by adding dormitories, to add more bed mattresses, to add tables and chairs into rooms so that they could write letters; and to pay wages to a medical orderly. He acceded to all the demands, but failed to keep his word. After another confrontation over a number of wagons to travel to the funeral on a muddy day, the members ended up walking and on their return, declared a general strike which Ruppin had to mediate. The manager Berman was fired and the workers' leaders also had to leave. This occurred in February 1911 (Shapira 43-44).

In 1911 at the 2nd Convention the 150 member Agricultural Workers Union of Judea established the socialized health care institution, Kupat Holim, literally The Workers Health Fund, or the Health Institution of the Workers of Israel which was a pre paid health service provider in direct response to the spread of malaria and the terrible facilities to care for the ill. In one statemen. It was explained that Kupat Holim "was created in order that the afflicted worker-and there is no human affliction greater than illness- should not be alone, neglected or forsaken" (Histadrut Program Problems Prospects 37). Due to the lack of any health services within the economic means of the workers, and the refusal of the farm-employers to extend health services to their employees, the Jewish agricultural workers decided to establish a health fund. From 1912-1915, two funds similar to the ones they had set up in Judea in 1911 were also established in the north and center of the country. In the first years, the health funds did not provide workers with medical assistance of their own. Only with the outbreak of World War I, were the health funds transformed from insuring companies into ones that provided medical assistance services. After World War I, it was administered by the two parties Hapoel ha-Tzair and Achdut ha-Avodah. Those funds existed side by side until after the establishment of the Histadrut in 1920. The Histadrut united them in 1921 and the health funds were amalgamated into a single organization–the Federation of Kupat Holim. (See the Review of Shulamit Reinharz in the Jewish Quarterly review 2006 of The Workers Health Fund in Eretz Israel Kupat Holim, 1911-1937 by Shifra Shavartz University of Rochester Press, Rochester, New York, 2002).

When Kupat Holim was first created, each member paid 10 mills dues, and the organization hoped to create a reserve fund of LP 24. In the beginning, it was supported by funds from the Keren ha-Yasod that helped it weather the terrible economic years of 1922-1927. After 1939, however, it balanced its income and expenditure accounts and contributions of the national funds was further reduced until in 1943, it only constituted 0.01% of the total income of Kupat Holim.

*Kupat Holim* began with the simple provision that in addition to minimal dues each worker must stand ready by the bedside of a fellow worker or send someone in his or her place. If necessary, a special room in Jaffa was rented as temporary quarters in cases where it was necessary to wait until a space became available in a hospital. There was an agreement to rent special rooms at first in the *moshavot* which contained many workers, at least in periods when sickness was widespread. The workers would also try to maintain a trained nurse for such rooms. From those meager beginnings a large network of moderately equipped expertly manned medical facilities were established covering the whole country. Thus, before the *Histadrut ha-Klalit* was formally established, the first of two major socialist need-based organizations had already been developed by a small number of workers (Kurland, 109-110).

In 1916, the Galilean Workers Union, one of many non-political workers' associations, established Hamashbir (the Crisis) the original Wholesale Cooperative which was given that name (during the period of World War I. Grain scarcity at that time had driven up the price of food, owing to Degania having felt the need to sell higher to attain a more profitable year than the two previous, as well as grain seizures by Turkish authorities. There was also less income available to buy food in places such as Kineret, and Gedud ha-Avodah had not yet contracted to work in quarries or build roads to earn more income for the collectives.

Thus, the purpose of *Hamashbir* was to allow workers to buy goods at consumer-cooperative prices. Interestingly enough, this cooperative became a consumer and a marketing cooperative. It arose out of necessity, as did *Kupat Holim*. It became the first one that the *Histadrut* would take under its wing four years later. Despite the fact that when *Hamashbir* was established in 1916, there were still two major parties with differing ideologies on how to organize collectives and cooperatives and a conflict did arise within Degania to join or not, it was just those strong willed ideologically leaders who had differed on many points (such as A.D. Gordon and others) who convinced Degania to become a partner in *Hamashbir*.

Almost forty years later, the Histadrut, which was the epitome of an industrial democratic institution, could brag that in one factory of 250 workers owned by *Hamashbir*, there were thirteen different countries, each with its own language and sometimes even a need for translators to coordinate the work process. At that time, (1955) the Histadrut figures for membership included 12.2 percent native born (Sabras), 58.3 percent of European origin,

1.0 percent American from the British Commonwealth countries, and 28.5 percent of Asian or North African origin (Near 45-46; Zweig 53).

Communal groups established during the middle of the Second Aliyah were different from the one established in Degania. One of them was the *Moshav Ovdim* or farmers' cooperative encouraged by Hapoel ha-Tzair and Berl Katznelson. Berl Katznelson advocated workers' settlements not as appendages to large colonies, but as autonomous smallholder's villages, where workers and their families could support themselves by cultivating their own farms. He proposed that Jewish labor be compulsory in the new settlements, or the *moshavim*, as they were called. To forestall the economic difficulties and resultant personal hardships of the early years in the settlements, he proposed that the members of the moshav be joint guarantors of the payment of the debts. This could only be achieved of course if the Zionist movement undertook the responsibility to settle the workers and allocate land to them. In order to prevent speculation, the land should be allocated on perpetual lease rather than on any principle of ownership.

The three principles which took hold by 1913 were: the workers plots were big enough to support them without the help of outside work; the land belonged to the Jewish National Fund; and the collective as a whole was to be responsible for its economic ties with the outside world (Shapira 52; Near 42).

By 1923, there were nine such *moshavim* (plural of Moshav), and they included within them a population of 534 persons. By 1927, there were 847 members in 17 Farmets Cooperatives (Near 80; 189). In 1914, Nahalat Yehuda existed in its embryonic form. Although between 1914-18, few Farmers Cooperative experiments succeeded, in 1921, Nahalal became the first permanently settled (Near 42; 69). During that year, Kfar Yehezke'el was also settled and six more *moshavim* were to be established by the end of that year. In some quarters, this was seen as a blow to the kibbutz movement. From Degania alone 60-65 members left to join a *moshav*. The existence of a new form of workers' settlement, legitimate in the eyes both of the labor movement and the Zionist movement, created practical, ideological, and political problems for the *kibbutzim*. It was postulated that economic problems were a cause for the social instability of the *kibbutzim*, as they'd been having problems even before the economic crises of 1923.

Some circles claimed that those problems were for objective reasons—the difficulties inherent in the 'conquest of labor' and the 'conquest of the soil': climatic conditions, meager accommodations, poor sanitary conditions sanitation, etc.. However, of equal importance was that in the earliest stages of

50

settlement they had relied on allocations from the Keren ha-Yesod (The Zionist Movement's Settlement's Fund) that was often unable to provide the required amounts to carry out its own modest plans (Near 94).

In the early 1920's, the leadership of the Settlement Movement was grounded in the cooperation of the triumvirate of David Ben Gurion, Berl Katznelson, and Yitchak Tabenkin. That cooperation usually guaranteed harmony within the party. However, in the years of 1923-1925, issues of the place of urban workers in the movement and the establishment by the *Hapoel ha-Tzair* of Moshav Nahalal created uneasiness among members of *Achdut ha-Avodah* that leaned toward the moshav form of settlement. It also initiated the developments which would break up the inner harmony of the three. In the early days, the *Achdut ha-Avodah* had regarded the large kibbutz as the ideal form of settlement, and the party was thus also enthusiastic about the Gedud ha-Avodah. However, in the mid-1920's, Tabenkin would be the only one who insisted that the countrywide kibbutz would encompass the whole country. In the meantime, in the early 1920's, Ben Gurion had warned the Nahalal settlers "You are sitting on the border. Beyond you, lies capitalism" (Shapira 155).

In the later years, the new form of settlement would be viewed as a positive development, but the unease and the ideological split by the mid-1920's would be a temporary dark shadow on the face of the pure socialism of the Settlement Movement.

The relationship with the Palestinian Arabs was an even more complicated issue for the Jewish settlers of the Second Aliyah, even though they vehemently opposed the exploitation of the Arabs and the Jewish workers in the colonies of Baron De Rothschild and in the original *moshavot* supported by J.C.A. The concept of Jewish labor was still viewed pragmatically; in order to gain a foothold in the country and reduce Jewish dependence upon the Arabs, at first the Jewish farmers had to employ their fellow-Jews. This nationalistic (Zionist) approach would dovetail with the socialist ideology of the Settlement Movement.

In the early stages of the Second Aliyah, 1905-1908, *Ha-Poel ha-Tzair* and *Poale Zion* each in its own way believed that the Jewish worker in Palestine would eventually evolve into a wage-earning proletariat. *Ha Poel ha-Tzair* believed that by appealing to the good will of the colonist farmers and by perseverance of the workers, Jewish labor would prevail. *Poale Zion* believed that the process would occur naturally, since the Jewish economy would expand through the investment of more Jewish capital thus creating more Jewish employment for Jews. Neither party had yet accepted that introducing Jewish labor into the colonies had failed. Even A.D. Gordon had not yet formulated his ideas on work as a value in and of itself. "His idealistic point of view of 'conquest of labor' as part of the general metamorphosis of the individual and society through the return to manual labor was not yet commonly accepted" (Shapira 38-39).

An early challenge to Jewish labor in the colonies was made by Yosef Vitkin who advised the workers to save money, buy land in the Galilee, and establish new settlements. He submitted his idea to Ha Poel ha-Tzair at the 1908 Conference and it was vehemently attacked. By the time Berl Katznelson arrived in Palestine, 1908, Vitkin had given up attempting to influence the labor movement, and it was in the throes of deep despair (my italics).

The worker could not compete with Arab labor and could not support themselves and their families working for the colonist farmers; what was left to do? The life of the colonist was considered by the idealists of that time to be degrading and contemptible, and tenant farmers on J.C.A. lands in the Galilee was proof enough of this. In the case of the first loyal workers such as Judean colonists since settling on the land twenty-five years previously, they had lost "all traces of the idealism" which had brought them to Palestine originally. They had been tempted to exploit Arab labor. On top of that, agricultural settlement entailed purchases of land and capital investment, and at that time, no worker could handle such a financial burden. Outside help would be considered charity. These factors created a difficult situation in the relationship with the Arab population, and the workers' own settlement's movement's potential (Shapira 39).

It wasn't until 1909 when Ruppin developed the ideas and the specific concept of kvutzot poalim that the change occurred. He viewed the socialist worker movement as a resource for socio-economic development. By this time, the experiments at Um Juni and Merchavia were under way. The Zionist Movement and Ruppin solved the issue of workers' lack of capital with loans which were received from non-socialist Zionist donors of Western Europe and the U.S.A. to workers who would thus not assume nor demand ownership of the land in the long run, but rather receive in a contractual way the land, tools, and farm animals (to a group of workers). They would continue to receive wages from the Zionist Movement (Near 35).

In 1908, Berl Katznelson had met A.D. Gordon, and in a discussion propounded his own ideas of a course to be pursued by Palestinian workers by which a new form of agricultural labor settlement where the workers worked for themselves without recourse to hired labor would be established. Secondly, according to Katznelson, the Jewish National Fund would purchase the land. Thus, Berl Katznelson felt that he was not only immune to the gloom of the period, but had created new hopeful schemes. Soon after that meeting, Ruppin the J.N.F. and the Zionist Movement arrived on the spot, and the kvutza became a reality.

In any case, from Herzl through Gordon, Katznelson, and Ben Gurion, and even to the days in England of the liberal Chaim Weizmann, the leadership of the pioneers and their supporters never dreamed of exploiting Arab labor, nor did they believe that there would be violence between the two peoples. Ruppin, Ben Gurion, Katznelson, and Weizmann never dreamed that they would declare a Jewish State in Palestine in those days, and it did not even penetrate the minds of their young Jewish European radical comrades that the Arabs who had been living for centuries in that desolate under-populated and practically ruined land could possibly object to becoming eventually a minority-a fully respected one that would live in more comfort and wealth under the most liberal regimes-through the massive immigration from abroad (Shapira 39; Elon 156-158).

The pioneers of the Second and Third *Aliyot* believed, in a romantic way, that the Bedouin culture resembled the ancient Israeli culture, even to the point where they believed that the Arab *fellahin* (peasant) was a direct descendant of the ancient Hebrews. This approach pictured them as shepherds, pressing olives for oil and using beasts of burden to plow. For these young pioneers, the Arab was a Bedouin shepherd or a fighting sheik (Frank, Ivan 43). In 1906, Shlomo Lavi visited two Arab villages in the vicinity of Jerusalem, one the Christian Ein Kerem and the other Moslem Colonia. He wrote then: "It is certain that their inhabitants are descendants of the ancient Jews. With the return of the Jews to settle among and around them, they will remember their true but and forgotten ancestry and come back to Jerusalem" (Elon 165).

Later a defense mechanism would be employed to protect the naïve innocence from being contradicted by fact. For decades they were served by the arguments that only the feudalists opposed; "the masses of people will soon realize their true advantage: objectively they are allies." Also helpful were utopian expectation that "progressive socialist forces in the Arab world" would lead to Arab acquiescence to their cause (Elon 157).

In many ways, they were viewing the Arab peasant and the Russian *Narodniki* through the same glasses as they had done in Russia, in regard to the peasants and the revolutionary party when they were growing up in the late 1890's. The Sabra workers who had grown up in the 1920's and in the 1930's,

53

reached the conclusion that they had lived for too long with the Arabs not to acquire some of their mentality (Zweig, 113). It is certainly true that in the years of the Second Aliyah, the pioneers at the worst were paternalists, while the best of their approach allowed them to be humanists, as they saw the Arab peasant as a member of–through no fault of his own–a sluggish and backward feudal society (Elon 164).

From 1908-1910, the British began to worry that anti-tsarist Jews would side with the rising young Turks and weaken the British relationship with Russia. Cited issues included their fear of a French style-Jacobin Revolution, the abdication of the Sultan, the rise of the Young Turks in the Parliament, alongside of only a few Jewish representatives–who actually were more anti-settlement in Palestine than some Turks, the C.U.P. which was the arm of the Young Turks' demands for liberty equality and fraternity, some Jewish influence in Salonika, and influence in the Free Mason Movement. Anxiety was created in the minds of the British of a conspiracy and a creation of a new Ottoman Empire or other developments in the region that would spell additional trouble for Britain. The possibility of an anti-Russian policy that would hinder British plans also came into play since the 'powerful' Jews were extremely anti-Czarist Russia (Fromkin 42).

> Although the only four Jewish parliamentarians in the Ottoman Empire behaved diplomatically and conservatively, there were still major British misconceptions, one of which was that Jewish influence wielded political power in the Ottoman Empire, and the World War in which by then the British were engaged could be won by buying the support of this powerful group; and its support could be bought by promising to support a Jewish homeland in Palestine. This was the turning point of the British position. Favoring the establishment of a Jewish homeland in Palestine, soon became part of the new approach of the British Foreign Office, and in 1917, it was pronounced in the Balfour Declaration (Fromkin 42-43).

In late 1914, the Young Turk Djemel Pasha tried to destroy the Zionist settlements, although lacking any rational reason to do so. He ordered the expulsion of all foreign Jews (Most of those Jews were socialist idealists from Eastern Europe who, while in theory remained subjects of the Czar, had come to Palestine fleeing pogroms and chose the hardships of pioneer life in barren Palestine over immigrating to America). Although the German Von Weigenheim and the American Henry Morgenthau interceded with powerful Turkish government figures such as Mahmed Taalat, the Minister of the

Interior of the Empire and Enver Pasha; and Ben Gurion and Ben Zvi, two Labor Zionist leaders who had studied law in Turkey opted to organize a Jewish Army to defend Ottoman Palestine, Djemel refused the offer and deported them. They immediately went to the U.S.A. to raise monies for such an army, and only late in 1918 did the five battalions of the Jewish Legion officially fight with the British Army against the Ottoman Empire in Palestine (Fromkin 210-211).

During that same period when the British policy was in favor of a Jewish State in Palestine, the French inaugurated a diplomatic and propaganda campaign designed to prevent Palestine from becoming "a Zionist State." The French were more opposed to a Jewish State than a British State in Palestine, since from their perspective, it would endanger their commercial and clerical interests. Fromkin's analysis was that in 1914 the French were the enemies of the Zionist Movement, more so than the Arabs (Fromkin, 17). The Quai d'Orsay, expressed itself in a refined manner, but the French papers expressed crude anti-Semitism; and the organization Oeuvre des Ecoles d'Orient, which represented French Catholic missionaries, claimed to discern a Jewish World conspiracy that sought to destroy the Christian World. One Robert de Caix, who managed French interests in Syria agreed, claiming that "The revolutionary and prophetic spirit which is so often found among Jews has turned to Bolshevism" amongst the Zionist Jews arriving from Eastern Europe. Thus the French saw their position in Syria and Lebanon threatened by a movement that they believed to be British, Jewish, Zionist, and Bolshevik (Fromkin 441-442).

The Zionists themselves continued to think that the little land of Palestine with its more than a half million non-Jews there would not be in the Arab nationalistic sights. However, even in the colonial period after the Histadrut was established in 1920, a growing Arab animosity did not allow them to be full members of the Histadrut, and Arab workers were organized separately in a movement linked to the Histadrut (Elon 165; Malkosh 21).

In the long run, however, the animosity which had occurred as early as 1908, and the riots that continued sporadically through 1921, were either ignored or viewed in the stereotype of European anti-Semitism by such outstanding statesmen as Yitzchak Ben Tzvi and Labor Zionists from Poale Zion. They even saw the free press attacks of the Young Turks as creating Christian articles that emanated from the hatred of European Christians who planted hatred in their co-religionists hearts. After the riots in 1920-1921, the Jewish leadership proclaimed that they had occurred because the Zionists had not made it clear to the Palestinian Arabs that their religious and civil rights would never be infringed upon (Fromkin 527).

There were some Jewish Zionists in the Diaspora such as Harry Sachar, one of the supporters of The Balfour Declaration, who warned the Zionist Movement that "Even if all our political schemings turn out in the way we desire, the Arabs will remain our most tremendous problem." (Elon 173) Beginning in 1919, the Jewish settlers themselves had begun to wake up, since gangs of armed Arabs periodically attacked the settlements. In the mixed cities of Jerusalem Hebron and Jaffa, Arab mobs brutally murdered women, children, and the elderly. Jews were also killed by marauders in the Galilee in 1920, in an area in which the British Army had not stationed troops (Elon 174; Fromkin 446).

Although the Zionists hoped to solve the problem by political means, by economic improvement, social change, education, maneuvering, patience, and the occasional negotiation, especially by charmers as Weizmann who did get to know the major Arab leaders such as Faisel in the period between 1916-1921, it did not change the attitudes of men such as the Grand Mufti of Jerusalem who in 1918 quoted the hadith: "Our rights are your rights and your duties are our duties" (Fromkin 446).

Weizmann had hoped that the Arab national aspirations would focus on a kingdom centering on the holy sites in Baghdad, Mecca, or Damascus, but they were interested in a Kingdom centering in Jerusalem. Their animosity stemmed "from emotion, religion, and xenophobia... feelings that that tend to overcome people when newcomers flood in to change their neighborhood" (Fromkin 523). Israel Zangwill wrote that "The Arabs should recognize that the road of renewed national glory lies through Baghdad, Damascus, and Mecca, and vast territories freed for them from the Turks and be content ... The powers that freed them have surely the right to ask them not to grudge the petty strip (Israel) necessary for the renaissance of a still more down-trodden people" (Israel 28).

By 1931, Weizmann apparently began to realize that the opposition to a state was growing, and he did hope to reach an accommodation by convincing the Arab leaders to make an agreement that immigration would be limited, and therefore the Jewish growth and expansion in Palestine would be so slow as to be hardly noticeable. Possibly, he also hoped that there could be an accommodation of a bi-national state, but in a few years the rise of Nazism made any restriction of immigration unacceptable to his fellow Jews as much as a bi-national state was to the Arabs. In 1931, only Ben Gurion's Laborites and a few of the General Zionists stood with Weizmann at the Seventeenth Zionist Congress in terms of not wishing to proclaim a Jewish State. He then resigned as President of the World Zionist Congress ostensibly for health reasons, but some historians claim because he was blamed by the delegates at the 17th Zionist Congress for not standing up to the British who were already limiting Jewish immigration in contradiction to the promises of the British Mandate. Zeev Jabotinsky, the chief proponent of declaring a Jewish State also resigned from the World Zionist Organization and then established the New Zionist Organization that evolved into the Herut Party and the present day right wing Zionist party, Likud. In 1935, when Weizmann returned, the situation had completely changed (Elon 176).

Following the Palestinian riots in 1936 and 1939, the British White Paper limited Jewish immigration to Palestine to 75,000 a year. At the same time, Nazi policy was to make Jewish lives as miserable as possible and to force them to emigrate. This was demonstrated by the Kristalnacht event in 1938. The Nazis were also planning the death camps. This British White Paper policy continued through World War II until the establishment of the State. The situation had become hopeless for finding a peaceful solution that would have included two nationalist movements living side by side in peace. Almost seventy years later, this concept of a bi-national state has been replaced by the moderate elements in Israel, including the left wing parties which admit that they need to be more pragmatic, and by the leadership of the Palestinian Authority, President Mohammad Abbas and Prime Minister Saylam Fayad with the more realistic goal of a Two State Solution.

# IV

## THE THIRD ALIYAH: THE PERIOD OF THE ROADS

*"Se'ee savev aynach ooree kulam nik'btzu" (Raise your
eyes and look around; they have all gathered before you)—
Isaiah 60:4*

Although the Labor Battalion (*Gedud ha-Avodah*) had ostensibly
disappeared by 1929, for reasons which will be discussed in detail in this
chapter, its role in the Third Aliyah was influential and considered a feature
which helped save the Settlement Movement from a potentially economic
crisis from 1919-1924. The European youth movement, Hechalutz's
immigrants from Russia, also played a major role in the Third Aliyah.

Although the period has been analyzed as a short one, and the inspiration
of the Bolshevik Revolution in Russia, which at first was seen as a driving
Utopian development by the young revolutionary Jews in Russia, did not
remain a burning flame for long (Whether or not this was because of
Bolshevik non-acceptance of the Zionist-Socialist participation in the new
Soviet governing operations, the Russian Civil War, and the pogroms during
that stage, or differing ideological attitudes toward the Comintern on the part
of Poale Zion, Tz'ir Zion, and the Achdut ha-Avodah is not completely clear,
but all have been discussed and analyzed in many sources) (Near 103-111;
Reuvsky 19; and Shapira, 109), the numbers of the Third Aliyah settlers did
tend to be larger and increase more so every year during that period than
during the Second Aliyah.

From 1918-1923, the population of the Yishuv increased by 39,000,
almost 8,000 per year, while the annual increase during the Second Aliyah was

only 3,000 per year. The factors that created the opportunity to settle in communes in Palestine included the role of the British in the Period of the Mandate, and the ideological and political leadership of such men as A. D. Gordon, Shlomo Lavi, Ben Gurion, Berl Katznelson, Yitzhak Tabenkin, and the hero of the famous battle at Tel Chai, Joseph Trumpeldor. Of course, the Histadrut (est. 1920) played a major role, as its institutions facilitated absorption and economic growth, as well as fulfilling its administrative mission of contracting work with the British authorities. But while this is so, it also faced ideological conflict with the organizers of the countywide kibbutz concept that prospered in Ein Harod and the rival majority group of the Gedud.

The Third Aliyah growth was stimulated by the absorption of small groups from outside the *kibbutzim*, called *plugot*, by the established socialist leadership that favored the 'one big commune' concept, as well as well as the labor movement's organization and dynamic development of the Gedud, which itself absorbed new immigrants in its own manner.

The young men and women of the pioneering youth movement Hechalutz began arriving in Palestine in 1918-1919, having risked their lives breaking the blockade barring roads from Russia, where they were organized, trained and selected. The movement had been originally conceptualized by Joseph Trumpeldor, who in 1920 would fall in battle with Arab marauders at Tel Chai in the Northern Galilee. Trumpeldor and his disciples in Hechalutz were constantly dreaming of large projects of collective enterprise to be carried out by labor in every field of agriculture, industry, construction, and transportation. Although the new immigrants did not receive the encouragement of Zionist leaders, who opposed to the "premature" aliyah, they did receive a warm welcome when they arrived from the workers who had settled the land. Although it was difficult for the Zionist institutions to absorb large numbers of the new members or even give them gainful employment, the young pioneers did have the same vision of work and settlement on the land as their predecessors. Moreover, many of them had not counted on help form the World Zionist Organization, and they did have the adaptability to take on whatever work or new projects that conditions might require or even suggest (Near 63; Kurland 15-16; Halpern 13-14).

After Joseph Trumpeldor's death, the numbers of Hechalutz members reaching the country increased, and with it the hardship they would experience when they arrived. However, there were two possible means of employment for them. The first was working alongside veterans from the Second Aliyah (predominately from 1904-1914) draining of swamps and settling in the newly-acquired J.N.F. land areas in the continuous section of land from Haifa to the Bet Shean area which included the Jezreel Valley. Secondly, they could through the leaders of the labor movement acquire work contracting with the British government to build roads and railway systems. The work included at first…"quarrying, stone-breaking, track-laying, masonry, and the like." Thus, work was subcontracted to groups of workers, living and working communally whenever the possibility of work presented itself and to wherever it would take them.

The new immigrants, the majority of whom were members of Hechalutz, joined the 'fellowship of the roads'. Hechalutz members lived in tents supplied by the Zionist movement or the central institutions of the workers' movement, ate in communal kitchens, and pooled their meager wages. Thus, from 1920 to 1922, the Period of the Roads was an appropriate name to give to the time when, six months after Trumpeldor's death at Tel Chai, a group of his followers met on the shore of the Kineret and founded the Labor Battalion or *Gedud ha-Avodah* (September 1920). "The ideology of communalism and pioneering fitted the historical development of the 'fellowship of the roads' and was the seed-bed of many developments in the kibbutz movement which came to maturity at later stages" (Near 65). To better understand the atmosphere of the lives of Gedud members at that early stage we can glean a few contemporary accounts.

> I went by horse and cart to the 23rd kilometer on the Haifa-Jedda road, where I was to join a work party. On the way, I passed young men and women, sitting astride bags of stones by the wayside, working with small hammers. By the side of every heap of stones, (stood) reed baskets for the gravel. Many of (the young people) had bandaged hands, and their faces and clothes were batherd in sweat, even though the sun was going down. Apart from them, the road was virtually deserted all the way. Not a Jewish village in sight-just the Arab villages in the distance, and ruins, concealing the secrets from the past (Near 65-66).

Although in most descriptions of the Third Aliyah and the role of the Gedud, road making was the central element (In *Land Policy in Palestine*, Abraham Granovsky states that between 1920 and 1922, there were 3,000 pioneers building roads), there were other types of work-building, laying of railway tracks, swamp-draining, and various sorts of agricultural work. Groups were made upon the basis of previous acquaintances, national or party or youth movement allegiance; but there was apparently a constant process of selection and groups were reformed and combined with others according to the type of work and relations between the workers (Granovsky 20).

A new vocabulary came into existence. "Kvutza" now came to mean a settled co-operative community on the pattern of Degania; whereas, the communal group with no fixed territory was called a pluga (plural plugot), and finally, a group of plugot with a common administration that grew up in 1921-1922 was referred to as a havura or a kibbutz. Gedud ha-Avodah, according to that terminology, was the first 'country-wide kibbutz'. By the beginning of 1921, it had the biggest organization of plugot in the country with some two hundred members. In the meantime, the newly established Histadrut took over from the contracting agencies of the parties and dealt directly with the British Mandate. All in all, by August 1922, there were 77 contracting groups comprising 2,044 workers (228 married couples and 380 children in the families). Gedud ha-Avodah alone had 186 members and three others had over 100 each. There were 17 groups with ten members or more (Near 67).

Of course, there had to be a good reason why such a type of contracting groups (plugot) came into existence and actually grew for three years. In that time period, there was a slow rate of agricultural settlement that was limited as earlier in the First Aliyah period by a straightened condition of Zionist funds. Nevertheless the expansion of agricultural *kvutzot* in the Third Aliyah was greater than in the Second Aliyah. There were 42 such groups in 1921 and 48 in the summer of 1922. Of that number, 24 were designated for permanent settlement as *kvutzot*; 76 of them had been founded during the Second Aliyah; 4 during the war; and 13 during the Third Aliyah (Near 68, Table 6). The numbers of members in the *kvutzot* grew from 1921 to 1922 from 600 to 1546. Interestingly, not only the number of *kvutzot* was growing during the Road Building Period, but within each *kvutza*, the number of members grew slolwly. The sector was growing on the foundations laid by Degania before World War, and even Degania which originally decided to remain small faced the increasing demand of intensive agriculture for more manpower. However, the majority of *kvutzot* followed Degania's original policy and remained small: Sixteen *kvutzot* had an average of 30 members or less.

> "The Gedud combined three separate and in many ways disparate elements: recent immigrants, mainly members of Hechalutz; Second Aliyah immigrants as Shlomo Lavi and Yitzchak Tabenkin; and members of the defunct defense group *Hashomer*. In the early satages, it seemed as if their common aims were sufficient to

61

outweigh the differences of background, outlook, and temperament" (Near 73).

However, the Gedud did become involved in a conflict that was complex not only due to the differences between the leaders as Ben Gurion, Katznelson and Tabenkin, but also within itself there were structural and functional differences. The first clause in its constitution said:"The aim: to build the country by creating a general commune of the Jewish workers in the Land of Israel" (Near 76). This notion was bold and translated into the idea that the *Gedud* would expand until it covered all of the Jewish working class and later into the 'common treasury.' Every *pluga* or kibbutz would work its own areas of specialty but would contribute its earnings into a common pool. The building trade workers of an urban *pluga* would build houses for everyone. This notion of one big communal centralized organization was opposed immediately by some of the stronger leaders, such as Shlomo Lavi. He believed that the big *kvutza* was viable and if it had land, capital, and manpower, it could be setup as Ein Harod was originally. However, he did reject the 'country-wide' structure of the *Gedud*.

Eventually, after a great deal of tension with the Histadrut's pragmatic, efficiency-minded leadership, Lavi and his friends of the Achdut ha-Avodah from the Second Aliyah, and the country-wide kibbutz followers backed by Ha-Shomer ha-Tzair drove Ben Gurion to form a commission of the Histadrut. This commission decided that the property of the two groups would be split, and the breakaway group would be called Kibbutz Ein Harod, which implied that it was a Federation of its three component parts, while the majority retained the name Gedud ha-Avodah (Near 77-79).

Berl Katznelson originally opposed the process of the 'country-wide' kibbutz, since his central theme, which he constantly hammered on for the labor movement, was unity above all else. He opposed the specific process of ideological collectivism begun in the Third Aliyah period, which was continued by Ha-Shomer ha-Tzair, a new European pioneering youth movement. This meant that the kibbutz was a collective body whose stand on political or social issues was binding on all of its members. In the 1930s, the movements, including Kibbutz ha-Meuchad, would be in a fight for the souls of the youth of Hechalutz with those ideological issues very much alive (Shapira 228).

Many of the *plugot* of the Third Aliyah were formed spontaneously and were part of the majority until 1928. They usually were formed on the basis of previous acquaintances or with the help of employment exchanges and the

Public Works Department of the Histadrut. Such loose federations of *plugot* were called *havurot*, working wherever they could, pooling their earnings, and eating in a common dining hall. They would receive monetary payment only if there was a surplus. Most of these young people did not come from youth movements and were never part of the country-wide movement (Near 134).

In the mid-1920s, Tabenkin and Lavi were in Ein Harod and they continued attempts to get the Histadrut Council to pass a resolution limiting the power of the kibbutz movement over its constituent members. Lavi gave up the struggle in 1926 when his group of supporters collapsed. Tabenkin was then able to become the leader of Ein Harod and promulgate his aims and distinguish them from the Gedud and Lavi. His central themes were the centrality of the settlement as an aim of the communal group and the idea of 'conquest'-the belief that the kibbutz movement should strive to expand the places and types of work of the Jewish laborer with limits fixed only by practical economic possibilities. In May 1925, the decision was made that Ein Harod was to be a 'country-wide kibbutz' (already comprising Ein Harod, Ayalet ha-Shahar, Yagur, and Gesher). It would spread over the north of the country and have *plugot* in several locations from Petach Tikvah to Jerusalem. By 1926, its rapid growth led it to surpass the membership of the Labor Battalion. Another important factor in its spectacular growth was that *Achdut ha-Avodah* chose to hold its conference in Ein Harod and made it clear that it (and thus the Histadrut) had chosen Ein Harod as its chief instrument in building the Settlement Society according to the theory of constructive socialism, the creation of a which would by-pass the capitalist economy, or eliminate it by competition (Near 145-146).

In Ludwig Lewisohn's book *Israel* written in 1925, Ein Harod was described as a heroic (and centralized) successful colonization effort of the *Gedud.* He wrote that during the previous three years (1922-1925 approximately), the colonization activities of *Keren Hayesod* had been centered on Emek Jezreel and the environs and the two types of settlement which grew were the moshav such as Nahalal and the *kvutza* of Ein Harod. The commune was situated by the spring of Harod which had been in an area full of swamps and the springs that abounded in that valley had overstepped their basins and old water courses and turned the land into marshes. The Arabs called the western spring *Ayn Samune* or Poison Well.

The Gedud had entered that area and turned the water of the springs into natural channels or pipes which gathered the swamp water into reservoirs; they discovered the western wells had been polluted by the sheep of the Arabs who were living in that area. The malaria that existed was stamped out and …"the valley then consisted (1925) of woods and fields and delightful villages. We stood beside the spring of Harod and saw it gushing from the deep cave in the hillside and leaned over and scooped up the water in our hands and drank." (Lewisohn 176-7) Lewisohn continues by saying that the Gedud had its central or governing council there, and the communism of the several hundred young men and women who live there was wholly unpolitical (Lewisohn 177-178).

Of the kvutza's branches, he lists farm crops, dairy and poultry husbandry, a smithy, a large carpentry shop which built anything from a beehive to a wagon, a tailor's a locksmith's and a shoemaker's shop. Other than those branches, there was a hospital, a small museum of natural history, a library of two thousand volumes, a children's house and a school. The centralization, as mentioned earlier, was very firmly entrenched. "The discipline within this strictly self-governing body is severe' His point was backed up by the fact that he wrote that the frequent occurring councils, "the work of the colony was planned and the concrete tasks assigned" (Lewisohn 178).

In the Third Aliyah, the situation radically changed in another way that is less commonly discussed. There were a substantial number of women in the kibbutz movement, and there was no longer any economic logic in confining them to women's work. Moreover, they created communes and kibbutzim not on the model of Degania but the idea of Degania, the model in which men and women enjoyed equality in all respects, including their right to participate in the 'conquest of labor.' Unlike their predecessors of the Second Aliyah, they arrived in the country imbued with the ideals of the youth movement that included complete sexual equality and the abolition of the bourgeoisie family (Near 87).

The philosophy of the youth movement was not only anti-familial, but also was backed up by the radical approach to the issue of employment. During the Period of the Roads, the veterans of Hechalutz set the tone, and the women worked side by side with the men in the stone breaking.

Therefore, when they finally found their places of settlement they eased into work in the agricultural branches. From photographs, verbal accounts, and writings of authors who were on the spot such as Lewisohn, it is now clear that women of the Third Aliyah were even more emancipated politically and occupationally than even there forebearers in the Second Aliyah.

Nachalat Yehuda, just north of Rishon Le Zion, started out with eighteen girls who started a collective with a loan of 450£. They immediately started a tree nursery, a poultry branch, and purchased a few cows. They were described as handling all the hardships because just as many other *chalutzim* and *chalutz*ot, they were the best in mind and body. They were also the most capable of high idealism and emotion, or, as a friend of Lewinsohn's explained it, "It is the spiritually sensitive who come here and brave these hardships and fling away life and health, for the sake of inner harmony" (Lewisohn 173-174).

From another perspective, although there was a rebellion against the earlier puritanical period in Palestine, often replaced by a relaxed atmosphere and a flurry of sexual activity once the kibbutz had settled on its own land, the nuclear family did become accepted or at least tolerated once the first child appeared. Although it was not emphasized, the bourgeois shtetl mentality remained. The husband and wife did not sit together in the dining hall or at meetings until the 1940s, but as one person put it in retrospect: "Below the surface we all wanted to be like everyone else in the world, and every girl looked for a boy to marry, even though formally there were no marriages" (Near 90).

The outstanding example of the faithfulness of the concept of the nuclear family is Yitzchak Tabenkin who became a major leader in Ein Harod and played a strategic role in the founding of Kibbutz Ha Meuchad. He came to En Harod with other Second Aliyah veterans and a wife and a child. Near believes that if there had been an attempt to abolish the nuclear family, it would have repelled him and other Second Aliyah veterans who played major roles in developing that kibbutz (Near 91).

There is no doubt that during this period of the Third Aliyah, the kibbutz movement's growth and stabilization was far greater than corresponding processes in the Jewish population as a whole. By the end of the Third Aliyah, the facts were pointing out to the members of the kibbutzim that the strength of the kibbutz and movement was on the increase, and it had laid a firm foundation of its own continued expansion (Near 91). In Berl Katznelson's book, The Kvutza, he suggested that there be a constitution to apply to every kvutza. Although the suggestion was rejected, it did show that the structure of the communal groups had become crystallized (Katznelson). Although the kibbutzim had many problems at the end of the Third Aliyah, including lack of agreement on the desirable size of their communities, its political connections, and relationship with the rest of the kibbutz movement, as a whole, kibbutzim felt they constituted a movement rather than isolated settlements. Amongst the troubling issues was that the major kibbutz movement Gedud ha-Avodah had suffered a blow when En Harod seceded, and from then on became a coalition of disparate forces (Near 95-96).

In both the *Gedud* and the *Ha-Shomer ha-Tzair kibbutzim*, there were many non-party members and those who opposed party activities, but there was also a minority of Achdut ha-Avodah members. In some veteran *kvutzot*, there also were members of *Ha-poel ha-Tzair*. Thus, there were already divisive tendencies that would continue to expand even though the underlying unity was the bedrock of the kibbutz movement's permanency (Near 96).

Tabenkin's all-out view of settling on the land and anti-bourgeois attitudes did in the long run help to establish the permanency of the kibbutz movement. By 1924, the word *kvutza* and other terms signifying communal groups had acquired fixed meanings. All of them had in common such elements *as common ownership and* management of financial affairs, *a general work roster*, communal consumption (food culture and allocation of clothes), and communal *child care and education*)" (Near 93).

By 1921, the British applied the policy of retrenchment to all its colonial possessions. In Palestine, there was a drastic cut made in immigration, at least partly due to the riots in Jaffa, and at the same time, there was a worldwide depression. By 1923, the virtual state of full employment became an economic slump. One area in which this was particularly felt was in the building trade, especially in Jerusalem. Jewish workers began to leave the country in large numbers; and only in the spring of 1924 was there a return to employment due to the growth of tobacco planting which not only gave many existing workers jobs, but even the needed work for the newly arriving immigrants (Preuss 71).

The *Achdut-ha Avodah's* intimate atmosphere was also evolving, with a declining emphasis on the *kvutzot* common during the Third Aliyah. During the Fourth Aliyah, which commenced in 1924, many chose to live in towns, causing them to become the center of absorption. Subsequently *Achdut ha-Avodah* became a more broadly based heterogeneous class party to which Berl Katznelson had aspired and which did emerge in 1930 as Mapai (the Labor Party). At that point in the history of socialism in Palestine, the urban workers became the majority. A new type of party activist came into existence-the municipal labor council representative; and the municipal labor council leaders reflected more and more the increasing influential party apparatus in the towns (Shapira 154).

The trade unionists like Berl Katznelson had a following in *Achdut ha-Avodah* and the separation of the *Gedud* and *Ha-Shomer ha-Tzair* (a youth movement originating in Europe) both with cohesive groups with their own leadership was not bridged, so there was not total unity during the Third Aliyah, nor even in the early days of the Fourth Aliyah, However, the strength of the urban proletariat and the labor councils eventually would outlive the *Gedud*, since labor institutions as *Solel Boneh* (the Building Corporation which contracted with the British and belonged to the Histadrut) eventually took over that sphere in which the *Gedud* had once reigned; *Ha-Shomer ha-Tzair* would, by 1948, become the backbone of *Kibbutz Artzi* and the followers of the pro-Soviet *Mapam*, and even in the 1920s, it was purely an agricultural movement.

Within the framework of colonization, the land purchases during the Third Aliyah were evenly balanced between town and country until 1930. By 1939, the Jewish National Fund, which had become the decisive factor in land purchases, had bought 1,356,200 metric dunam of land in Palestine. However, Arab opposition to land sale resulted in price hikes that made post-WWI land purchasing more difficult. The Arabs did this because they viewed the Jewish purchases as encouraging the numerical increase of Jews in Palestine. Also factors were their seeing the purchases as the British violating the conditions of the Mandate, as well as their own tendencies to give far better prices to Arab purchasers than to Zionists. The land-purchasing situation after the War coincided with the Arab riots of 1921, even though the sales did stabilize the Arab landowners' and tenants' material conditions. The Palestinian British Mandate government passed measures to protect the Arab tenant farmer and those private Arab farm owners who existed, and this policy also made purchasing land more expensive and complicated (Granovsky 6-7; 10; "The Land Question in Palestine" 1).

After World War I, the Jewish pioneers tried to buy the land with the best soil. Gradually, this became possible with the introduction of more profitable crops and the application of better farming methods on land previously considered impossible to cultivate. This evolution held true for the Arab lands as well. The Arab peasants (*fellahin*) at first considered only heavy soils such as the ones that were suited for cereal crops to be worth cultivating. They did not have any idea how to work the light soil of the coastal plains. As a result of the spread of citriculture, that soil became the most valuable in Palestine. In terms of population, after 1920, the available uncultivated land showed a significant shrink, both as a result of the expansion of Jewish settlement, and the rapid growth of the rural Arab population. The census of 1922 counted 366,500 Arabs in the rural areas, and by 1931, it had risen to 533,800, a 45.7 % increase (Granovsky 4; See Tables, I and IV; Granovsky 11: 28 on Proportion of Rural Population to Total Population and Real Estate Transactions in Palestine).

The Third Aliyah had produced the crystallized *kibbutzim* and the countrywide movement; although it was more difficult to purchase the richest land, the land areas were cultivated in an efficient manner. The Jewish attempts to help the Arab *fellahin to* expand their agricultural production by learning new methods to use for different types of soils fell by the wayside. Arab nationalism and the British change of heart led to the British retracting their promises in proportion to Arab resistance, as the Jewish population increased. The immigration to the towns also stabilized the Palestinian Jewish economy, and the Histadrut's non-union activities such as its enterprises began the development of the country economically. It soon would be politically in control, as the *Gedud ha-Avodah* slowly died out during the Period of the Road.

# V

## THE GENERAL FEDERATION OF LABOR: ORIGINS OF INDUSTRIAL DEMOCRACY

*"Poale Zion helps the Histadrut (General Federation of Labor) in Palestine in its struggle to safeguard and to promote the interests of labor in private, national, and governmental enterprises."—From a speech by the Director of the Histadrut in Pittsburgh, Edward Steinfeld*

On December 4, 1920, eighty-seven men and women delegates representing the 4,433 Jewish workers throughout Palestine, in a hall attached to the workshop of the Technion in Haifa, gathered to effect the unification of the Jewish workers in Palestine. The struggle that had been going on for a generation, the struggle built on slogans and the worship of words was about to end, and the *Histadrut* was about to be established (Kurland 3-5). The eighty-seven delegates to the Conference were divided according to proportional representation into the newly formed United Workers Movement or Workers Unity (Achdut ha-Avodah), 38 delegates; *Hapoel ha-Tzair,* 27; Newcomers (*Hechalutz, Ha-Shomer ha-Tzair*), 16; and the Jewish Socialist Workers Party or Poale Zion Left Wing, 6 (Kurland 22; Preuss 61).

The unification of the Workers Movement (*Achdut ha-Avodah*) began in 1919, and there is no doubt that Berl Katznelson and David Ben Gurion were the driving forces behind the negotiations which established the new workers' movement in the spring of 1919 at a Conference in Petach Tikvah (Preuss, 57). This beginning of the workers' movement's unification led to the Conference which a year later established the Histadrut.

69

On the surface, Ben Gurion and Katznelson would appear to have come from two different viewpoints to socialism. Ben Gurion was a follower of Ber Borochov and Marxism, while Berl Katznelson was loyal to individualistic subjectivism of the First Russian Revolution and to Berdichevsky's philosophy of the Will. However, although they came from two different approaches to socialism, Ben Gurion had concluded that his objectives were identical to Katznelson's after reading his article "Facing the Days Ahead" (Shapira 84). After all, it was Berl Katznelson who had seen unification as the natural outcome the organic development of the movement, the corollary of internal trends and of the true will of the workers in Palestine (Shapira 82). Thus, *Achdut ha-Avodah* had planned to combine the roles of party and trade union, an association of autonomous trade unions rather than a party whose members were to remain loyal to a certain credo.

The latter concept was mainly due to Katznelson's approach, since he was averse to dogmatic socialism. Although in this formulation was a touch of syndicalism and a dash of Kropotkin, the original desire was to construct a social-political—trade union organization of the widest possible basis. (Shapira 82; Near 64-65). In the platform of Achdut ha-Avodah, was "socialism insofar as its orientation was towards the workers and its vision was of organizing non-class society. It bore little resemblance to any socialist theory" (Shapira 89). In essence, the founders of *Achdut ha-Avodah* set themselves the objective of developing Palestine, and its political structure was based on a rather strange blend of centralization and decentralization with the cells envisaged as trade unions, while the central body of the association was to be elected at a general conference of all the workers. Ben Gurion had also made three demands and two of them were incorporated into *Achdut ha-Avodah's* program: participation in the World Alliance of *Poale Zion* and participation in the Socialist International. The third one, the principle of class struggle, was not accepted (Shapira 88-89).

When the Conference to form the Histadrut met in Haifa in December 1920, after only a few days of violent debate and amidst great rejoicing, the *Histadrut* was established. It was unification on the basis of a single comprehensive organization for all workers. Its activity comprised the trade union, settlement, and economic, social, and cultural fields, with political activity left to the parties. All existing trade union and institutions were merged and neutralized (Preuss 61). The trade unions formed part of the General Federation of Labor that officially soon became known as *Histadrut ha Klalit*. The latter's General Convention would be elected on the basis of proportional representation. At the elections, each party, group or trade union would be entitled to put forth its own program. At this juncture in 1920, there was established a central agricultural office as an organ of the united agricultural organization; a "Public Works and Building Office" to take charge of work of this kind (later known as "Solel Boneh"); unified labor exchanges and immigration offices; a cultural commission; a sick fund; a workers' bank; a consumers union; unified trade unions, and urban labor councils elected by the whole labor community of the relevant town. The conclusion was that finally there was an organization that was really capable of absorbing immigration and guiding it into the paths of productive work (Preuss 61).

By the time of the Second Histadrut Convention in 1923, a depression had set in and in between 1920 and 1923 other factors hindered the development of the Jewish Labor Movement in Palestine. However, in 1923 the basic Constitution of the Histadrut was written. It included the following, which defined its purpose:

> The Histadrut (General Federation of Jewish Labor in Palestine) unites all workers who subsist on earnings of their own work and who do not exploit the labor of others, in order to provide for all communal, economic and cultural matters relating to the working class in Palestine with a view to the establishment of a Jewish laboring community in the country. Membership is open to all "male and female workers of eighteen years of age and over who subsist on the earnings of their own labor without exploiting the labor of others and who agree to abide by the rules and decisions of the Histadrut" (Kurland 40).

The statements above did contain within themselves what distinguished the Histadrut as a trade union movement. The Histadrut became unique in many respects in the breadth of its organizational base, the scope of its activity, and its internal structure.

From 1920 on, the Histadrut embraced the whole of the labor movement. The parties continued to exist but the Histadrut took over the administrative responsibility for many of the tasks that they had previously dealt with separately and in competition (Near, 65). It certainly was governed by a series of coalitions, but the United Workers Movement had the majority from the beginning. In 1922, Ben Gurion became the Secretary of the Histadrut and he remained so until 1930. In May 1929, the *Hapoel ha-Tzair* and *Achdut ha-Avodah* parties, which had remained split due to ideological differences, merged and out of that union, Mapai, the Eretz Israel Workers Party of which Ben Gurion remained the head for over three decades, was born (Shapira 162).

By 1925, the Histadrut united all its cooperative institutions in a "Cooperative Associations of Labour" better known as Hevrat Ovdim (Preuss 98). That organization from the beginning had overall social and juridical functions. Around the same time, the Public Works and the Building Office were united into one corporation "Solel Boneh." The agricultural settlements were organized under a cooperative roof, Nir (Furrow). By 1930, the non-profit organizations listed below all belonged to Hevrat Ovdim: Nir, (Collective Furrow) which was the legal framework of settlement, Solel Boneh (public works and building corporation), Hamashbir, the consumers cooperative (Tzarhaniya), Yakhin, the Workers Bank, Tnuva, the company for the marketing of agricultural produce, The Workers Educational Stream, Hassneh, the workers' life insurance company, Merkaz ha-Cooperatzia, the Central Office for producers cooperatives, and the Shikun, the urban housing office. Also the cooperative Eged was established to provide transportation between Jewish settlements.

At the same time, non-economic institutions were established such as the workers' education center and the cultural commission. At this time, the special unions as the Women Workers' Council, and the Youth Workers' Organization came into existence. Finally, there were two other popular organizations set up: the sports club network (ha-Poel) and the workers' theatre, (ha-Ohel) (Preuss 98-99).

The major advantage to the labor movement in setting up *Hevrat Ovdim* was that there now was a centrally located institution in the shape of the Histadrut' s trade union center, while the national branch unions (the agricultural, building, transportation and other unions) together with various local groups and labor councils looked after branch work. On the other hand, until 1924, there was no *de jure* overall organ for the labor community's cooperative sector, but only separate cooperative and collective institutions such as *Hamashbir*, the consumer cooperative, the Workers Bank and *Solel Boneh*, public works and building office, which operated separately and independently of each other. In setting up *Hevrat Ovdim*, at the Second Histadrut Convention, the Histadrut brought about a change in that respect (Preuss 179).

However, what was even more utopian-sounding but which actually remained until the present as it was originally established, was the fact that the *Hevrat Ovdim* existed as a blanket organization for all of the Histadrut's economic enterprises and institutions whether cooperative (managed by the members—"All the members of the Histadrut automatically hold membership of *Hevrat Ovdim"*) or administrative (managed as a subsidiary enterprise by a *Hevrat Ovdim* administration), "it entrusted to its extensive tasks in the economic and settlement field, in the towns, and on the land and at sea, and in the air." Although it did sound utopian and fantastic then and even now, it did all come to pass. The full extension of the resolution and the establishment of the functions of *Hevrat* Ovdim did create something different from everything known in the world labor movement. In the first sentence of the resolution, the concept is defined: establishes full extension of the Histadrut as *a trade un*ion organization and Hevrat Ovdim as a holding *company* for economic enterprises. In 1965, Walter Preuss wrote:

> The daring novel structure of *Hevrat Ovdim* has fully vindicated the hope of its founders i.e., their aim to create *a* blanket organization, active in all fields of the economic and settlement build-up which should coordinate the work of its subsidiary enterprises and provide leadership in the spirit of pioneering work of the Israeli labor community (Preuss 180-181).

One must add that the Histadrut Constitution also spelled out such matters as the relations between the individual member and the Histadrut, and rights and obligations. A wage scale was established for all Histadrut enterprises, based not on vocational skills, but on *the size of the wage-earners family* (My italics) (Shapira 127). The idealistic creator of *Hevrat Ovdim*, David Ben Gurion summed up the Histadrut by stating first what it was not before defining the breadth of its organizational base, the wide scope of its activity, and its internal structure:

> The Histadrut is not a trade union, it is not a political party, it is not a cooperative, nor a mutual aid society, although it is active in all these fields; it is more than all that. The Histadrut is a union of people who are building up a new home, a new State, a new people, new enterprises and settlements and a new culture; it is a union of social reformers which is not rooted in its own membership book but in the common destiny and tasks of all its members-in death or in life (Preuss 182).

Ben-Aharon referred to the new formulation years later as an "Industrial Democracy." Ben Gurion defined the Histadrut as a national democratic-socialist institution established by a democratically elected group of volunteer leaders who would administer trade unions, cooperatives, and holding companies after being elected by the workers themselves, workers in a land they dreamed would become their homeland and their State. These workers would also provide for themselves and all workers, and relate to each other as fellow workers in terms of income needs, health needs, and all other needs of all the citizens who worked whether in towns, villages, cooperatives or the kvutzot and kibbutzim. Therefore, membership was not just a list, but the lives of all the workers.

There is not any doubt that the Histadrut was established in a democratic fashion and was a socialist federation of labor which in its structure and actions not only provided for all its working population social justice and equality, but also provided the democratic means to have a voice in all decision making. In *Cooperative Palestine*, Samuel Kurland points out that the workers at the end of the Conference in December 1920, left the hall in Haifa "united into a single democratically constituted federation" (Kurland 39).

The Histadrut united all workers who subsisted on earnings of their own work and who did not exploit the labor of others, in order to provide for all communal, economic, and cultural matters relating to the working class in Palestine. It also served another purpose: to be the anvil upon which the renascent Jewish people were to be forged. The workers were not to leave to the employers the question of the quality, nature, and productivity of the worker or his constant adjustment and adaptation to the national goal. All of these had to be their concern as well. Out if that reasoning sprang the wide organizational base of the Histadrut (Kurland 42). This also led to the breakdown of all distinctions between one type of worker and another, and to the inclusion of all of them within the same organization as equal partners with the same collective responsibility.

Thus, the Histadrut from the beginning comprised all workers without distinction Jewish or Arab, urban and rural. After the establishment of the State, there were 89,000 Arab members in the Histadrut; and as early as 1938, the effort was being made to form unions of Arab and Jewish workers together. Although this task was difficult to accomplish so early on, especially under stress of the pogroms of Arab gangs in Hebron and Jerusalem, there were some Arab-Jewish relations. They were, however, limited to British government services as in the ports and railroads or in conjunction with companies such as Shell Oil. These relations and one joint Railway, Postal, and Telegraph Workers Union were most meaningful in Haifa (Revusky 35-36).

The Histadrut's Chevrat Ovdim also contributed 500,000 mils to the Arab Workers' Peasant Fund, and made other investments and laws for Arab cooperative ventures, consumer agricultural societies, village development, and irrigation societies. (Malkosh 58). By the mid-1950's, there were 100,000 Histadrut women workers in the economy, in agriculture, industry, and the professions. There was also an autonomous movement dealing with the special needs of women and promoting welfare projects (Malkosh 106).

One of Histadrut's goals is expressed by the phrase '*the protection of all hired workers*' who join the Histadrut. This did include veterans and newcomers, Jews and Arabs, skilled and unskilled. (Malkosh, 21) In 1912, many years before the Histadrut was established, there were already two urban producing cooperatives in Haifa, and by 1936, there were 76 urban cooperatives affiliated with the Histadrut, under the auspices of its Workers' Cooperative Societies' Auditing Union (Reuvsky 52-53).

The Histadrut did not make political distinctions, and it was open to all political parties, and every worker regardless of his or her political views and party affiliation. Members were not obligated to belong to a political party, but if he or she wished, they were free to join. Therefore, there have been differing political views amongst the rank and file, and politics (as everywhere in Palestine and after 1948 in Israel) plays an important role in the organization. Any group with 100 supporters could submit a list of candidates for election to the Convention, and based on the numbers of votes it received send delegates to that Convention. The parties in their drawing up of the party lists do try to give adequate representation to all sections of the working community. (Malkosh, 24) For example, in the 1945 election, the Labor Party had 53.7%, The Unity of Labor Party Zionists 17.7%, Left Poale Zion 20.7%, General Zionist Workers Party 3%, Yemenites 0.5 %, New Immigrant Workers 3%, the Peoples Workers Revisionists 0.2%, Religious Workers 1% and Unattached 0.2% (Kurland 45-46).

The organization of the Histadrut is framed from the bottom up: The first stage in the Histadrut organization is the Workers Committee at the place of employment. The Committee is elected from time to time by all the workers employed in the particular establishment. The second stage is the local trade union that embraces all the workers of a specific trade. The third stage is the local Labor Council in each town or village. The fourth stage consists of the country wide federations and organizations such as the Agricultural Workers' Union, the Union of Clerks and Office Employees, the Union of Engineers, Post and Telegraph Workers etc., and the last stage is the Histadrut organization, consisting of the General Convention to which delegates are elected once in three years, and the General Council which serves as the supreme body between sessions of the Convention (Kurland 46-47).

The democratic nature of the Histadrut is exemplified by its wide base of decision-making. Since every member of the Histadrut is also a member of the *Chevrat Ovdim*, the Histadrut's Conventions are empowered to decide in *all* questions, whether in the trade union sector, or the cooperative sector, so that in practice, wage earners who are members of the Histadrut can have a say in questions pertaining to the cooperative sector and vice-versa e.g. members of settlements, and of other cooperatives, although they are not wage earners, can have a say on wages (Preuss 180).

The Histadrut absorbed every class of people into the socialist sector. Every member of the Kupat Holim was also a Histadrut member, and technically speaking, the only membership dues in the Histadrut were collected by Kupat Holim. The Kupat Holim members even referred to them as Kupat Holim membership dues. Technically, Histadrut members received free health service through Kupat Holim. Thus, Histadrut membership had growth driven by all the people, not just the working class.

In the early 1940's, Robert R. Nathan made an exhaustive study of the Histadrut and concluded with this remark: "Its affiliates and own institutions dominate the fields of mixed agriculture, contract construction and road transportation...The labor movement is energetic, creative of new enterprises and new forms of social organization, decentralized, abounding in parties and doctrines and full of active surging life" (Kurland 43-44).

> The fact that the workers have collective responsibilities and that the Histadrut was always inclusive and its workers hold direct membership and enjoy equal rights (not a federation of unrelated trade unions bodies differing in wealth and in power according to the income from members' dues); and the fact that it is creative and energetic-having various parties and differences in their doctrines which they espouse does help negate the grave danger of to any workers' community-passivity of its members to a larger goal and the interests of the community as a whole (Kurland 44).

Thus, the above aspects of the Histadrut were able to combat the danger of passivity that could jeopardize hard-won principles of democracy. Aharon

Becker the Secretary General of the Histadrut in 1962 expressed the goal of a workers' democracy when in his report he stated:

> The drive to increase the workers' participation was not that labor and management each speaks for separate interests, but that they achieve full cooperation for the advancement of common interests; to ensure the future of the labor economy, to increase the workers' sense of responsibility by buttressing their status, and to attain that industrial democracy in which workers would regard themselves not only as wage earners but as participants in the creative enterprises (Becker 9-10).

The volunteerism of the workers' community from the years of the Second Aliyah also is a prime example of the initial democratic socialism which was developed by the same pioneers who created the Histadrut in Palestine.

In 1938, Abraham Reuvsky wrote that the leaders of the Histadrut were proud of the fact that every *kvutza* founded in Palestine was the result of the free initiative of its members. The members of the kvutzot chose the communal basis of their collective farms, not because of pressure or even persuasion from above, but by their own free will (Reuvsky 47).

After it was established in 1920, the Histadrut helped organize strikes against private enterprise in the towns and in small cities. The first strikers mostly consisted of regular laborers who opposed owners who exploited their labor. Only one strike occurred in 1919, but between 1920-1929 strukies numbered 260 with 7,825 strikers participating—the victories tallied to 167, the defeats to 43, and 47 where compromises took place. In the 1920's, 67% of the workers were in the building trade, agriculture, industry, and handicrafts, while before immigration only 28% were involved in those types of work. Once they reached the country, 38-39% of immigrants became involved in those works (Preuss 43-44).

In the 1920s, the Histadrut was so strong that 93% of all labor positions were part of the Federation while *Hapoel ha-Mizrachi*, the religious workers' party, had the other 7%. Thus, there was not a role for strikebreakers. In 1948, private enterprise had to face the Histadrut and the strikes, but within Histadrut-owned industry such as Koor, the largest agency of heavy industry in the county, there were workers councils and workers' management; and the same institutions existed in Solel Boneh, The Construction Company, Hamashbir ha-Merkazi the Central Wholesale Society of the consumers' cooperative movement and Tnuva, the Central Marketing Agency of the

77

agricultural settlements. By the mid-1950's, thirty of the Histadrut enterprises were managed by the workers (Malkosh 81). It was then truly a Workers' Democracy and the need for strikes in those industries was non-existent (Becker 110-114; Malkosh 76).

As early as 1946, *Kupat Holim* had serviced almost one half of the Jewish population, including workers of the religious *Hapoel ha-Mizrachi* that by 1959 claimed seven percent of the organized workers but did not have its own union, or its own health services. It also serviced thousands of Arabs from the dues and assistance of the workers' community (Kurland 107-108; Zweig 239). By 1946, there were 288,145 members of the Histadrut, 46% of the population of Jewish Palestine (Kurland 107-108). By 1960 there were 1,380,000 members and 9,454 employees, and there was a listing of 923 dispensaries, 17 convalescent homes, 280 laboratories and pharmacies, 30 x-ray institutes, 45 institutes for physical therapy, and 192 infant welfare centers. The total number of beds available in nine general hospitals was 2,000, and cases of protracted diseases were placed in seven special hospitals. Kupat Holim was servicing 100,000 people daily (Kupat Holim in Israel Report 1960).

Due to political changes in the government when the right-wing Likud Party gained control of the Coalition government in 1977, the Histadrut's industrial ownership was diminished to the utmost degree. In 1949, Histadrut had owned in output a tenth of the country's manufacturing industry. By 1990, it did not own any major industries.

The democracy of the Second and the Third Aliyot was emphasized by the patterns of the *kvutzot* and *kibbutzim*, which began as close-knit undifferentiated groups controlled by a system of direct and universal democracy. Gradually that pattern became more formalized, as was the case with the meetings. What was once the long meeting that began on a Friday and lasted until late Saturday morphed into the General Meeting once a week on Saturday evening.

The basic patterns of accountability of the officials and the frequent general meetings remained unchanged. In the earlier period, at least until 1930, the official organizational posts-treasurer and farm manager did have long term tenure, but by the early 1930's the principle of rotation, so much a part of kibbutz life in the Twentieth and Twenty-First Centuries came firmly established.

78

Another example of the Third Aliyah struggles to retain an open, democratic society occurred when in the Gedud ha- Avodah (The Labor Battalion) kibbutzim, a more centralized system took hold. In that system, committees were elected from the plugot and from the large kibbutzim as Ein Harod to the central bodies of the Gedud movement. These were far afield from the participatory democracy of the early kvutzot. However, in the Gedud ha-Avodah settlements with larger numbers of members, there was a weekly central meeting. On the day-to-day running of the farm an elected committee appointed people to various tasks, such as treasurer or work organizer, and those in charge of productive branches.

In contrast to the Labor Battalion the youth group of *Ha-Shomer ha-Tzair kibbutzim* were more democratic and close-knit. They also shunned the anti-intellectual attitudes of the Labor Battalion that ostracized a well-known poet, Avraham Shlonsky, who had been an accepted member after he had organized their sports field. In general, the *Ha-Shomer kibbutzim* members lived together, had myriad cultural activities, and even kept communal diaries. Their tendency was toward a more cultured behavior than the Labor Battalion. By 1929, the relatively small Labor Battalion completely disappeared, its 195 members to a commune in the Soviet Union, Vita Nova, and the right–wing faction of 294 members in 1926 merged with Kibbutz ha-M'uchad (The United Kibbutz Movement).

# VI

## LEADERSHIP: IDEOLOGY & LIVING ON THE LAND

*"They shall plant vineyards and drink their wine. They shall till gardens and eat their fruit. I will plant them on their soil, never more to be uprooted."—Amos 9:14-15*

The leadership of the Second and Third Aliyot has already been discussed as one that consisted of young mostly single men and women. These young men and women had studied Hebrew and Yiddish in the hederim of the Russian Pale, and were in one way or another involved in their teens in revolutionary movements and Zionism. Their ideological differences in Palestine may have been sharp in regard to each one's style of organizing the kvutzot, the kibbutzim, the Labor Battalion and the Histadrut, but the similarities in the upbringing and the attitudes in Europe of Berl Katznelson, David Ben Gurion, Yitzchak Tabenkin, A.D. Gordon Dov Ber Borochov, and Manya Shohat do stand out. Although the ideological perceptions of a few of the above leaders may have differed; in essence, they were all Zionists and democratic-socialists who lived that ideology completely in their everyday lives in Palestine.

The leadership of the six mentioned men and women in the political, ideological, and self-fulfilling physical labor spheres (Gordon called it 'conquering labor') enabled the establishment of the first self-sufficient democratic and socialist collectives in Palestine. This chapter will outline their early lives, their values, and their ideologies.

# Berl Katznelson

Berl Katznelson (1887-1944) was one of the most striking figures of the Second and Third Aliyot. Katznelson, known and beloved by all of Palestine when he died, was born to a Zionist family in Belorussia. The entire family was Zionist and belonged to *Hovevei Zion*. His father was a merchant and a Maskil (enlightened Jew), who endeavored to provide Berl with a good Hebrew Jewish Education. However, Berl actually received most of his education by his own efforts. His house was a large library where he spent most of his younger years.

Berl later tried out various political movements and parties of the period. This was the period, after all, of Herzl's political activity, the first Zionist Congress, and the controversy over Uganda as a potential Jewish State. It was a period rife with pogroms, which were not halted by the 1905 Russian Revolution.

In 1900, Berl's father died. He tried to help his mother by learning how to become a People's Teacher (a tutor). He eventually became a teacher of Jewish history in Yiddish-Hebrew Literature and was responsible for the Hebrew Yiddish library in a school for poor girls.

It was this time in the teaching profession that helped him to meet other learned people. At that time, Berl Katznelson was close to the Samists, who believed in establishing autonomous Jewish institutions in the Diaspora which in turn would lead to territorial concessions. At other times, he was close to the "territorialists" who supported the Uganda Plan. In the end he dispaired at the majority of doctrines and platforms he encountered, feeling they had no substance or course of action. Of this situation he stated:

> I don't know if our fathers who were inflicted with waking up at nights worrying till after midnight about their plight and forgot there with the general difficulties and bitterness of the Diaspora have ever alienated themselves from the calamities and shame of our people to the extent we the confused youngsters of the revolution have. We have absorbed the pain of all the world: the wine of the revolution has intoxicated us; its armies we have served; in its most stormiest have we excelled and in its failure we fell apart (Merlstein 3; "Berl Katznelson, 1877-1944").

Since the events of 1905 made clear that pogroms would not cease, and the Russian Revolution would not create a democratic and tolerant society in a recently defeated monarchist Russia (the Russo-Japanese War), Berl also declared:

> "We have justified ourselves and defended our tradition to and apart, like the tradition of children who were away from their fathers. While awake and in our dreams we have seen the blade of the sword, the physical decline and the spiritual burn a real danger of spiritual extinction has followed the Jews in the wake of the Revolution of 1905-an alienation from the people, negligence of the Hebrew language and culture and likewise, the Jewish people became a desolated island from which the youth disappeared. What was the way out? At this time (1905), an abandonment of the Hebrew literature has prevailed. One was completely disappointed with Hebrew; Hebrew books were no longer published. I was sitting then in a group of teachers and writers in the neighborhood when a copy of Brenner's Ha Meorer arrived. In this group were sitting people who had been Brener's readers, but also have the audacity to say, "Look what this man is doing, such an important person like Brenner, on what is he wasting himself' (Merelstein 4)?

Berl claimed that he saw at that moment how people who grew up with Hebrew literature were removing themselves from the issue.

> I left the meeting and resigned from the group, and said no to myself. For me the issue is over, not from the point of view of reconciliation with the ones who compromise over Hebrew." On that day I secured my final decision, be it in regard to Hebrew or be it in regard to *Eretz-Israel*, I say it again: not because of Zionist belief but because I am insulted, and out of stubbornness and because of refusal to be part of a generation which doesn't even have the strength to die with honor (Merlstein 5-7).

Berl apprenticed to a linker, saved money and became an immigrant in 1908. He arrived that year in Jaffa and was enraged by the conditions of villages, poverty, and dependency of village workers on overseers armed with whips and more eager to hire cheap Arab labor. These injustices led him to discuss and soon favor collective land purchases by the Jewish National Fund to protect workers from the arbitrary abuse of the landowners. Further, it allowed for the managing of colonies which would become self-sufficient. This led him to Kineret, a kvutza in the Galilee near the Sea of Galilee (Lake Kineret) where he became the mainspring of the strike against the overseers. He was the one chosen by his fellow workers to represent them in negotiations with Arthur Ruppin, the Director of the Palestinian Bureau of the Zionist Organization ("Berl Katznelson, 1887-1944" 1).

Berl Katznelson who made aliyah out of disappointment in the Diaspora was not only a leader for self sustaining work on the land, but also ending the disunity that immigrants brought with them from the Diaspora. During this early period, Berl was in a dream world with Joseph Brenner and A.D. Gordon, "a period of dreams" about the emergence in the Land of a Jewish workers society. Later he described that early period thus:

> "Numerous things have happened of the sort of "*Yomtov*" (A good day) every day that brought me in our land, wonderful things of the sort we experience but wouldn't recognize and won't be able to feel; the sort of the ever present wonderful mystic called "Eretz-Israel" (Merelstein 8).

The proclamation of pioneering Zionism was written by his mentor, Berdichevsky. Using Berdichevsky's terms, he wrote in the first article which he wrote in Palestine in Mi Bifnim (From Within) the following:

> "The legacy or our forefathers, the suffering of generations, and the ravages of history are gradually giving away though in the teeth of considerable opposition- to the *new forces rebelling against* them. A change of values approaching...a change in matter and spirit" (Shapira 15).

After World War I, Berl endeavored to unify the workers of Eretz-Israel around three principles: Zionist Socialism, *Chalutzism* (pioneering including agricultural training as a means to succeed), and the Hebrew culture. Until about the mid 1920s he had strong connections to A. D. Gordon and Brenner. However, this was not matched with Yitzchak Tabenkin and the Cultural Zionist Achad Ha Am. The latter he believed was too optimistic, and thus dangerous, respecting independence and cultural growth in the Diaspora, even under the dictatorial Czar.

The first two principles guided him the most and led to some conflicts later, especially with Yitzchak Tabenkin over different attitudes and issues of unity within the Labor Movement. (For more details on the many conflicts between these two intellectual and spiritual giants of the Second and Third Aliyah see Merlstein, 9; Shapira 31-33; 230-231; 258; Near, 223-224; 350. These pages describe in more detail than the previous Chapter VI (The Third Aliyah), their conflicts in regard to how these two men viewed the workers of the Second Aliyah and Third Aliyah, as well as their perceptions of the Labor

Movement's absorption of new immigrants and the power struggles that occurred within it).

Berl Katznelson claimed leadership of the entire labor movement or at least of all the people in his own party, *Achdut ha-Avodah.* However, the idea of unity, which was for him the organizational principle, drove him and to seek leadership, though paradoxically not through a bureaucratic system. This is contrasted by Tabenkin, who used the Kibbutz ha-Meuchad movement to gain authority in the labor movement.

Berl's authority flourished in an open framework, but in the large movement, based on pressure groups and power struggles, his influence was not felt. His main values were integrity, frugality, simplicity, and mutual aid and he exhorted others to these values. He established them as norms in the conduct of leaders of an entire generation, and if someone faltered he was there as a living reproach (Shapira 348-350).

In a final analysis of his values, and ideology Berl Katznelson remained throughout his career "the spokesman for what might be called the Romantic component in Labor Zionism."(Wolfe, Robert 238)

> He was greatly beloved and was considered by many historians to be one of the few people close to Ben Gurion. He and only he was referred to as Ben Gurion's "comrade and teacher" (Shapira Foreword VII; Ben Gurion, Selections 8).

## Ben Gurion

The most well-known of the six leaders in the early modern Palestinian period was Ben Gurion. Although his name and his career are famous, he was not a messianic leader nor did he knowingly seek to establish a cult of personality. There was never a particular 'ism' nor ideology ever attached to his name. In fact, although he was a Labor Zionist, the Labor Zionist manual never mentions his name, though the 1946 manual mentions Joseph Brenner, Ber Borochov, and Berl Katznelson.

Ben Gurion carried no factional label with him until very late in his career. In her autobiography, My Life, Golda Meir wrote that he was "one of the least approachable men I ever knew." She also wrote that "you had something specific to talk to him about, some business to conduct with him or you didn't go to him. He didn't need people the way the rest of us did" (Wolfe, Robert 231-232).

On the other hand, in his autobiography, Amos Oz the famous Israeli novelist, wrote about his being summoned to meet with Ben Gurion in 1961 at 6:30 A.M., while the writer was in the regular army and a kibbutz member, just because he had penned (respectfully) a response to one of Ben Gurion's philosophical treatises in the Histadrut Davar newspaper. In it, the Prime Minister and Defense Minister said that equality between human beings was impossible, although they could achieve a measure of fraternity. Oz recalls in his autobiography being so nervous the night before that he couldn't sleep and admitted to praying silently the whole night for an earthquake, a war, a heart attack—"his or mine, either would do.: According to Amoz Oz, Ben Gurion's detractors ridiculed the cult of personality surrounding the Old Man, but his admirers saw him—- "as The Father of the Nation, a sort of miraculous blend of King David, Judah Macabee, George Washington, Garibaldi, a Jewish Churchill, and even the Messiah of God Almighty" (Oz 439).

Ben Gurion was born David Green or David Gruen in Plonsk in the house of his father Ezekiel Green, a *Hovevei Zion* member. When he made Aliyah in 1908, he began to write letters to his warm Jewish community and even then he told of hunger and malarial fever and of physical labor in the day and of the night guard duty in the midst of complex ideological discussions and political debates. He also honestly discussed home sickness. In *Selections*, Brakhah Hadas wrote that even then "his words were imbued with Jewish and Zionist vision and ardor which are characteristic of Ben Gurion to this day (1948)"(Ben Gurion 7). In 1915, he wrote, "Not with money, nor by privilege, but by our own acts will we win a Homeland. We will receive it not from the Peace Conference or the nation that rules it, but from the hands of the Jewish worker who will come to take root in it, to bring it life and to dwell in it" (Ben Gurion 6).

Because of his ideals and his strong character, Ben Gurion, in 1936, was the one man who could unify the *Haganah*, the self defense underground, the armed descendants of the *Shomrim* which were secretly established in 1915, and the *Palmach*. He was the virtual commander of the pre-State army, even though he was not a man of war. He wielded no weapons. However, Ben Gurion knew well that before there was a Jewish Army, there had to be a Jewish economy, and by necessity the economy needed to be based on socialist principles.

Ben Gurion prepared himself for his career in Turkey before the outbreak of World War I where he studied the language and the laws of the land. He was already training himself for the political function which he had envisioned (Ben Gurion, *Selections* 7). Ben Gurion, who changed his name from Green, or Gruen, based on the defense leader's name in the Jewish Rebellion against the Romans (70 C.E.), shaped and crystallized the pioneering community in Palestine. No one had by 1948 or even to this day contributed as he did to Zionist affairs in his assumption of responsibilities vital to the political establishment of the State of Israel.

Ben Gurion lacked personal charm but "he built his authority in the corridors of power, first as Secretary of the Histadrut then in the Zionist Executive." (Shapira 348) As a leader he was able to attain the most intense concentration of ardor, the utmost clarity of resolution, and retain the peak of his abilities from the time he arose as one of the major Socialist Zionist leaders in the Second Aliyah period until the State of Israel was established in 1948. One writer claimed that it was no accident that he had the titles and duties he assumed when the state was established (first Prime Minister and Defense Minister), since the fitness of the thing was self-evident (His leadership in the Jewish Agency and the Histadrut in Palestine leading up to that served as proof). "There is no other man among the Jews who symbolizes so fully the values alive in Israel in 1948 and in the Hebrew revival."

One important aspect of Ben Gurion's character and value system was that for him the fate of the Jewish people was rooted in its spiritual values. He had no liking for the Mensheviks or the Bolsheviks, and he was certainly not a follower of Trotsky or Lenin. In fact, he once criticized Trotsky's "No Peace, No War" remark. He did love the *Tanach* (the major source of the writing of the Prophets), and he was known to have said things such as, "We follow the Biblical Mandate not the British Mandate" during the time when the British attempted to curtail Jewish immigration during World War II and immediately after it. In actuality, he was only interested in Jewish revival, as his fight against Nazism and The Mandate simultaneously would clearly display. He was always an idealist first and never understood that there was a possibility that a Jewish person in Palestine would not be an idealist.

Ben Gurion's most important achievement was the ideological victory that came with the founding of the Settlement Society, a viable socialist and democratic society established during the period of the Second and Third *Aliyot*. Shortly after the Third Aliyah period ended, Ben Gurion wrote in retrospect that what the Second Aliyah pioneers found in Palestine, with the idea of the 'conquest of work' on their minds, were not any Zionist funds, nor any real dreams of Jewish colonization by the workers. In fact, the term 'National Ownership of Land' was not commonly used in the vocabulary of the workers. What they found was that the twenty-five existing settlements were maintained by private enterprise and hired labor. He further stated that the greater part of the capital came from individual donors as Baron de Rothschild and the majority of hired labor was not Jewish. He claimed also that there were even ideologues who attempted the boycott of the Jewish Worker on political grounds. The phrases "the workers regime" and the "dictatorship" were not yet popular amongst the middle class, but still no change had taken place in the nature of the Jewish worker (*Selections*, Ben Gurion 10).

However, in 1932, he was able to point out that the Jewish working class had been established in country and city. The workers were building suburbs, cities, the roads and the highways.

"We find them in the quarries as stone masons, digging ditches, boring wells, handling and carrying goods. We find them in every kind of work in field and garden, in every branch of trade and industry. There is no field of work into which the Jewish worker has not penetrated" (Ben Gurion 10).

In that same year, he wrote that Tel Aviv was a household word "not because of Jewish shops or Jewish banks or Jewish mayor—you will find such in many places—but because as no second city is, it is a metropolis of Jewish labor" (Rebirth, Ben Gurion 47).

### A.D. Gordon

Perhaps one of the most intriguing figures of the Second and Third *Aliyot* was Aaron David Gordon (A.D. Gordon). It is no wonder that the foreword to his essays emphasized that Gordon grew up in a wealthy Orthodox family molded from *the* day of his birth by fields and forests in an obscure, *Troyano*, *village* and lived his adult life in the famous Galilean settlement of Degania. He was always in close proximity to nature, and philosophically has been identified by more than one Labor Zionist author as being the Jewish heir of Tolstoy. "Gordon's approach to *Eretz Israel* as the 'Mother of Nations' whose image is reflected in Jewish culture and the Hebrew language (and therefore in each Jewish soul) contains a spiritual potential for a profound understanding of the link between the Land and the people of Israel"

This perspective reinforces the analysis that Gordon's type of nationalism and Zionism widely known as the "religion of labor" was truly an original idea. It emphasized the moral aspects of 'the conquest of labor' and laid stress on the connection to the Land of Israel by which the Jewish worker, through his physical labor and direct contact with the land, would be regenerated. Gordon felt that the Jewish youth had to conquer labor for his or herself and conquer the Jew for labor. For Gordon, that meant overcoming the prejudices against physical labor so deeply rooted in a landless people. The prejudices would have to give way before the new concepts of the dignity and love of labor. Gordon stated it in the following way:

> A people that has become accustomed to every mode of life save the natural one-the life of self-conscious and self-supporting labor—such a people will never become a living, natural laboring people unless it strains every fibre of its will to attain that goal. Labor is not merely the factor which established man's contact with the land and his claim to the land; it is also the principle force in the building of a national civilization (Kurland 9).

Gordon's actual influence stemmed more from his personal example working the land (although it was not at all easy for someone his age To live off of the equivalent to 6 kopeks a day) and his quasi-paternal relationships with the young workers of Palestine (He did sing and dance with them and always displayed a cheerful personality) than from all his writings of that time period (Ramon 1; Near 17; Shapira 33). In one of his writings, Gordon exclaims that "The first thing that opens my heart to a life such as I have not yet known is work. Not work for a livelihood, not work in obedience to a command, but work upon which a new light shines" (Hoffman 85).

As a son of a wealthy merchant he received a thorough, private Jewish education in the Talmud with a certain amount taught of the Hebrew language and with the Bible. He was frail of body, but had the will to learn Russian, German, and French on his own as well as learning Hebrew. However, writing in 1938, E. Silberschlag wrote that "...the poverty of thought, the meagerness of original research, the imitation of Biblical phraseology and diction in short the defects of peculiar to our national literature during the greater part of the nineteenth century disgusted and repelled him."

Gordon, at first, neglected Hebrew literature, as did many of the early Socialist-Zionists. Achad Ha Am, however, affected a different attitude in him, even though in later years Gordon criticized the well-known Cultural Zionist because he had a small understanding of Palestinian labor (Gordon XI).

Due to connections as a relative of a baronial family, the Gunzburgs, 'A.D. Gordon', as he was known by many in the Labor Zionist movement, did not have a problem attaining a good job as an official on one of their estates. For 23 years he remained at the position, although he had not the necessary virtues of mediocrity and adulation. As his family grew to seven children, he educated them, and in doing so his own interest in education grew. Slowly he became the intellectual center of the village and neighboring town and began to give lectures, arrange readings, and have debates on Saturday in his synagogue. He preached that brand of Zionism called Hibat Zion (The Love of Zion).

In 1903, after the estate was sold, Gordon decided to make *aliyah*, but first he was sure his family was taken care of properly. Only two of his seven children had survived. One of the two, a son, was independent. The daughter was teaching, and therefore could help her mother; and he left some monies from his inheritance at the disposal of the whole family (Gordon 12). In 1904, at the age of 48, Gordon, who became the doyen and the teacher of the workers of the Second Aliyah from Russia to Palestine, made Aliyah. After five years working the land, he brought his wife and daughter to Palestine. (Hoffman, 84) "Despite his age, he took his place with the workers and rapidly became one of their spiritual leaders" (Near 17).

It was not a whim that drove him to the soil where he remained until six months before his death from cancer. He stated unequivocally that he would meet death with joy if he could work on a farm to his dying day. His conviction, which he elevated to a philosophy that had practical implications for the pioneering members of the early Twentieth Century, was that the Jew must weed out economic parasitism, redeem his land by manual labor, and his spirit by contact with the soil. There is no doubt that A.D. Gordon was the 'spiritual' mentor of Democratic-Socialism in Palestine or of Labor Zionism (*Labor Zionist Manual* 19). His kvutza Degania was considered "the Mother of all Kvutzot."

Gordon did not perceive any hierarchy in nature; to him the cyclical characteristics of nature exemplified the philosophical principle of lack of hierarchy and that this principle provided a duplicable model. Against nature stands the modern urban culture which is mechanical competitive and therefore alienating (Ramon 3).

In the last ten years of his time in the Galilee, he became an almost legendary figure but never exploited his preeminence by asking for special privileges. Although he would have preferred to work in Degania until the day he died, his life ended in Europe after battling cancer (Gordon xiii).

## Dov Ber Borochov

Dov Ber Borochov has been called a Marxist Zionist, and he was the founder of the Labor Zionist movement as well as a pioneer in the study of Yiddish as a language (He published in The Record, "The Tasks of Yiddish Philology", 1913). He was born in 1881 in the town of Zolotonosha, Ukraine to cultured parents; a father who taught Hebrew and eventually moved to New York, and a mother who possessed a love for learning and sparing no effort to educate Dov (Ber Borochov 11). Ber Borochov not only read extensively, but he made sure he understood every word before putting it down. At age 11, he entered the gymnasia and by the time he graduated (1900), he knew Greek, Latin, Sanskrit, Philosophy, and Economics. Because his father was a teacher, he was protected from suspected participation in revolutionary movements. However, he did read illegal literature during this period (Ber Borochov 12-13).

Gordon had always been considered a leader by Jewish and non-Jewish friends, even those who were much older than he was. As a young adult, Ber Borochov joined the Russian Social Democratic Labor Party but was expelled in 1901 because of his Zionist beliefs. He then organized a labor club with Socialist Zionist leanings, and was a traveling lecturer of the General Zionist organization. In 1903 he wrote his first treatise, "The Nature of the Jewish Intellect."

By 1905, he was a member of the Poale Zion Party and then helped form that party in Russia and in America, including helping to formulate the 'Poale Zion Program.' Due to numerous splits, however, the pro-Palestinian Poale Zion Party only had its first convention in 1906 and that program guided the party until the Bolshevik Revolution of 1917. Ber Borochov was arrested in June 1906, but even in prison, he was able to set up a "Peoples University," and there Ukrainian socialists fell under his nationalist spell. Later, some Ukrainian Social Democratic groups called themselves "Borochovists." After his escape to Minsk, he studied Yiddish until forced to flee and become a wanderer in Europe and America. (13-14) His fame occurred in Zionist circles and in Labor Zionist circles because he was able to explain nationalism in general and Jewish nationalism in particular in terms of Marxist class struggle and dialectical materialism. He believed and expounded on the idea that "the class structure of European Jews resembled an inverted pyramid where few Jews occupied the productive layers of society as workers" ("Ber Borochov" 1).

Ber Borochov also believed that when a nation finds itself in an abnormal situation, without its own territory, all sectors would rally around the national struggle. This approach justified for him his Zionist ideology.

One of the most interesting historical facts about Ber Borochov was that he has been glorified as one of the two Labor Zionists (The other person was Nachman Syrkin) who believed that the Arab and Jewish working classes had a common proletariat interest and would participate in the class struggle together once Jews had returned to Palestine ("Ber Borochov" 1; Ber Borochov 124).

The above two Labor Zionists were also considered the major theorists of socialist Zionism in Europe. It is not difficult to comprehend that Ber Borochov was credited with influencing many Jewish youth to immigrate to Palestine from Europe. According to the Labor Zionist handbook, the Russian *Poale Zion* program followed closely his theories that included (as mentioned earlier) "non-proletarization." That theory that was fully developed by him and by Nachman Syrkin was also claimed by the brilliant unifier Katznelson. To remind the reader what this theory advocated, let us add that it was intended to convince Jewish socialists that the Jewish people in the Diaspora could not make the transition from lumpen proletariat to true working class status ("Ber Borochov"; Shapira 13; *Labor Zionist Manual* 10).

In Our Platform, in which he was advocating Palestine as a National Home (He referred to it as Eretz Israel), he made the point that the economic activity of Jewish immigrants would tend to lose its industrial and commercial character and to turn towards producing the means of production and towards agriculture in a land such as Palestine. However, most of the Left Poale Zion ideas of Dov Ber Borochov were untenable in Palestine by the 1910's because it was a struggle for the pioneer settlers to establish an economic foothold on the land, and there was a need for inter-class cooperation.

Ber Borochov's followers in Eastern Europe and Palestine, however, did continue to vigorously support class struggle and support the Bolshevik Revolution. When he returned to Russia in 1917, he also did so (*Labor Zionist Manual* 10; Ber Borochov 1). However, while still in America, Dov Ber Borochov proclaimed in a letter to his Central Committee that he was still a

Social Democrat unlike his Russian *Poale Zion* party, which was now supporting the Bolsheviks. His comrades described that analysis as exaggerated, and he did speak at the Third Conference of the Russian *Poale Zion* movement. In that famous speech in 1917 which emphasized the "Jewish Nation", he said, "When we say Jewish Nation we know that it has existed even before the class division in modern society. We also know that the proletariat at one time will constitute the nation and that the working class is the one that creates the nation."

The new terminology gave expression not only to Borochov the thinker but also the man of sentiment. "Therein he proclaimed his faith in the Jewish cooperative colonization movement; he proclaimed anew the belief in Jewish Nationalism" (Ber Borochov 124). In the speech itself, besides proclaiming the belief in Jewish Nationalism, Borochov was specific in his analysis of both Socialism and Zionism as compatible.

> Socialism has several aspects. Economically, it means the socialization of the means of production; politically, the establishment of the dictatorship of the toiling masses; emotionally the abolition of the reign of egoism and anarchy which characterizes the capitalistic system. And so it is with Zionism. Economically, it means the concentration of the Jewish masses in Palestine; politically, the gaining of territorial economy; the striving for a home. Recent times have witnessed a desire on our part to give expression to these emotions. And we need not fear what our neighbors will say... (Ber Borochov 125-126).

According to Ber Borochov, the goals were different twelve years previously, since the battle had then to be fought against the Bundists and the General Zionists. Although he was able to convince the Convention to adopt his point of view, the further developments of the Russian *Poale Zion* widened the schism between followers of the old Borochov and the adherents of the author of "Eretz Yisrael in Our Program and Tactics" ("Ber Borochov" 1).

In time, the Left *Poale Zion* and the Right *Poale Zion* (those who appreciated his older theories and the other faction which accepted his new position) became modern Israeli parties *Meretz-Yachad* and Labor. The Left *Poale Zion* was effectively destroyed in Europe by the Nazis and persecuted later by the post–war Communist regimes.

Dov Ber Borochov died in 1918 but remained famous both for his inverted triangle concept, and his democratic and socialist ideology, joining together the Jewish and Arab proletariat, and the Socialist-Zionism with which

Zionist youth movements later identified, with which Ben Gurion's Mapai Party clung to, and to which the modern *Poale Zion* Party in America readily hitched its ideological wagon.

## Yitzchak Tabenkin

Yitzchak Tabenkin, 1887-1971 was well known as one of the founders of *Kibbutz ha-Meuhad kibbutz* movement and the *Achdut ha-Avodah* party, and he was a member of the First and Third *Knesset* (Parliament). He was also known as one who created splinter groups or factions which led to the development of two major left wing parties after 1948, *Achdut ha-Avodah* and *Mapam*. He was one of the leaders of the non-party group in 1917 that created *Achdut ha-Avodah* (Labor Unity) and established the *Histadrut ha-Klalit's* foundation at the first Conference in 1920. That all-encompassing labor movement and administrative body was a final compromise of two parties, *Ha Poel ha-Tzair* and *Poale Zion*.

Tabenkin was born in Bobruisk, Belorussia in 1881, and was raised in a religious family in Warsaw. As with many of his contemporaries, he studied in Warsaw, Vienna, and Berne. He gave up religion to become a student of Marx and the Hebrew poet Bialik. In Poland, he helped to found the *Poale Zion* and was from the beginning a strong supporter of the Land of Eretz Israel and the settling of agricultural collectives. In 1911, he settled in Palestine and worked on a farm. He also joined *ha-Shomer* (the Guard). Tabenkin advocated collective settlement and used the term "communist settlements", later giving up the term because he did not accept the Soviet approach to communism. (Gorenberg 15)

He joined the same *kvutza* during World War I in which Berl Katznelson had lived, *Kvutzat Kineret*. After World War I, he became a member of *Gedud ha-Avodah* (The Labor Battalion) and helped to establish Kibbutz En Harod. Tabenkin always favored large *kibbutzim*, which would be open for mass membership. In essence, he was a populist and not an elitist (Rolef 417-418).

In 1917, Tabenkin was already in the leadership of the Labor Movement and at that time of stress economically, a non-party group including Tabenkin and Katznelson felt that the traditional parties Poale Zion and Ha Poel ha-Tzair had enough in common to unite. By 1919, the first attempt was made for the unification of the labor movement, and it was in the form of a new labor movement, The Achdut ha-Avodah labor movement (Labor Unity) which was intended to be a comprehensive framework for all those who embraced Labor Zionism. At its first conference, Tabenkin gave the programmatic address. However, as many members of Hapoel ha-Tzair wished their party to become stronger with the arrival of new immigrants, the only Labor Movement people who joined The Achdut ha-Avodah were the non-party members, ex-members of the Poale Zion, and a few of the Ha-Poel ha-Tzair faction. Therefore, at the beginning of the so-called 'period of the roads' during which Gedud ha-Avodah (Labor Battalion) members were active workers on the infrastructure of Palestine, the minority group contracted separately from the Achdut ha-Avodah (Workers' Unity) with the British for labor, and had separate administrative machinery for the absorbing and supporting immigrants, labor exchanges, sick funds, Hebrew classes, and printed material.

In the end, this duplication of administration for a small number of workers led to the realization that one administrative body was necessary; and in 1920, Tabenkin was a founding member of that comprehensive body the *Histadrut ha-Klalit*. Despite the fact that the two parties continued to exist, the Histadrut took on administrative responsibility for many of the tasks that they had dealt with separately and in competition, and it was governed by coalitions of which The *Achdut ha-Avodah* remained the majority. This party continued to dominate the labor movement through the administration of Ben Gurion, as Secretary of the Histadrut beginning in 1922.

In 1930, the Mapai Party was established uniting the two former parties. Yitzchak Tabenkin was also one of the founding members of Mapai (Near 64-65). Tabenkin, however, clashed with Ben Gurion and others in the mid 1920's over the issue of whether a kibbutz such as Ein Harod would be a 'country wide kibbutz' which would spread over the entire country and absorb smaller groups such as *plugot*, and eventually be the only type of communal settlement to absorb all new immigrants. The Histadrut wished more individual *plugot* to be established to absorb immigrants and opposed Shlomo Lavi's (the other leader of the *Gedud ha-Avodah*) idea which advocated the opposite. At that juncture, Ein Harod had become independent of the *Gedud ha-Avodah*, which would begin to die out by 1926. After a struggle, Shlomo Lavi gave up his point that the *plugot* should all be absorbed by the one kibbutz, and thus Tabenkin, the other major Gedud leader, arose as the leader of En Harod.

Tabenkin supported the idea that the kibbutz movement should expand the places and types of work of the Jewish laborer with limits fixed only by practical economic possibilities. In other words, he supported the 'conquest of labor' and the centrality of the kibbutz settlement as the aim of every communal group, but not only in terms of communal settlement and 'conquest of labor,' but in terms of culture and education as well. Those were the two major issues on which he focused.

During the dispute of 1921 over the role which Hechalutz, the Zionist youth movement, and their mentors *Kibbutz ha-Meuchad* had in training of pioneers and distributing immigration certificates, Tabenkin, representing the Kibbutz Movement and his view of the position of Hechalutz, rejected the administrative position which it was given. They saw it as an educational framework destined to include the other movements and to ultimately supersede them. Since in their eyes, this was bourgeois in origin and in conception, it would ultimately cause unnecessary divisions in the kibbutz movement. In Tabenkin's own words, "anything which reminds (a kibbutz member) that he is of "bourgeois" origin that his culture was once Hebrew or Yiddish or Polish or Russian-reduces our own stature and weakens us" (see footnote 48, Near 129).

Tabenkin believed that the working class of the Settlement Society and within that working class, the kibbutz must be united by abolishing distinctions of origin and culture which other youth movements were determined to preserve. To Tabenkin, this was the purpose of the kibbutz and its youth movement during the time of the preparation for the pioneers' new life. Hechalutz and the *Kibbutz ha-Meuhad* represented the general interest of the Histadrut and the working class as a whole. Therefore, he believed that they should be acknowledged as the overall framework for the preparation and the absorption of pioneers. This was the concept of '*klaliut*' (Near 129).

By 1925, it was decided that Ein Harod was to be a 'country- wide kibbutz'. In fact, then it was a combination of farms including Ein Harod, Ayelet Hashachar, Gesher, and Yagur scattered over the north of the country and of *plugot* (small groups of workers) between Jerusalem and Petach Tikvah. By the end of 1925, Ein Harod actually had 515 members; more than 22% of the whole kibbutz movement and in 1926, with a spontaneous influx into the kibbutz, its membership at 607 had surpassed the Gedud. Ein Harod had become the colonel of the new *Kibbutz ha-Meuchad* movement.

Tabenkin's concepts contained a seed of opposition with their ideological kibbutz "holism.' Tabenkin and Lavi saw the workers suburbs for the new immigrants also receiving agricultural land and becoming part of the 'country wide kibbutz;' but even more important being the only communal settlement to absorb such workers; whereas, Ben Gurion, who was responsible for the management of the Histadrut and the *Achdut ha-Avodah* party, did not agree. He and his circle believed that the kibbutz should not be the only way to absorb immigrants and not be the only communal farm to develop the land. He believed that *moshavim* and *kvutzot* were necessary and should be part of the Histadrut structure (Near 146-147).

In regard to the above issues of the role of Ein Harod, the 'country-wide kibbutz,' being the only communal settlement type, *Kibbutz Ha-Me'uchad* and *Hechalutz*, and the overall absorption of young pioneers by them, Ben Gurion and Katznelson clashed with Tabenkin. However, these principle disagreements were not the last between the intellectual and spiritual leader of the Second Aliyah. In many respects, Tabenkin's *'klaliut'* and anti-'bourgeois' positions also put him in direct opposition to the great Cultural Zionist Achad Ha Am. For Achad Ha Am, the settlers' souls were more important than the number of settlements.

In 1937, in opposition to the first proposed British partition plan, Tabenkin "advocated settlement in all corners of the country as part of keeping Eretz Israel united, and he fought for political activism, and the independence of the Histadrut." In 1944, when Mapai split he led the faction known as *Ha Tenu'ah le-Achdut Avodah* which joined with *Ha Shomer ha-Tzair* to form *Mapam*. However, he always fought against the left-wing element of the party which was empathetic to the Communist Bloc, and in 1954 became the leader of *Achdut ha Avodah-Poale Zion* and was elected to the Third Knesset. In 1960, he retired from politics and party life and devoted his time to teaching and writing. He was a delegate at every Zionist Congress after World War I and headed the Seminar Center of *Ha-Kibbutz ha-Meuchad* at Efal. He remained in Kibbutz Ein Harod until his death in 1971.

## Manya Wilbushewitz Shohat

Manya Wilbushewitz Shohat was born in 1880 on an estate in Western Russia, in an area called Lososna, near Grodno. Her father was wealthy, deeply religious, and unlike many of his contemporaries, he was interested in technology. He had a mill that employed many peasants. His wife was not at all interested in religion. Manya's mother who had a secular education also was vehemently against Manya's brothers becoming rabbis. Therefore, in the end all of Manya's seven brothers and sisters managed to seek their own ideological path, not staying on the estate to accept the roles their parents wished for them. One became a Social Revolutionary terrorist, one joined Hovevei Zion and immigrated to Palestine, one became a Tolstoyesque peasant, and one obtained a superior technical education and became an engineer in Palestine. Several committed suicide when their feminist, romantic, or social ideals disappointed them. Manya herself was at first profoundly religious and then equally committed to the peasants. At fifteen, she ran away to Minsk, and in her brother's Gedaliah's factory had her first experience in trying to improve the working conditions of agricultural and industrial workers. Manya eventually organized a strike of five-hundred workers against him (Fuchs 60-61).

As a teenager, Manya Shohat was drawn to many ideological groups, became close to the Bundists, members of Poale Zion, *Hovevei Zion*, Social Democrats, and the Social Revolutionaries. She also was able to absorb aspects of each group. At first she acted to establish study groups where she taught literacy, economics, and socialism to the workers. On one relief effort which she joined in the Tartar region, she helped to bring economic and medical aid to peasants suffering from the drought and cholera. There, she learned the advantages of the Russian *mir*, or Russian communal system. As a newly committed socialist, she set up an urban collective on her return to Minsk. Collectives, she believed provided—"proletariat with the means of struggle" (Fuchs 61).

Manya was arrested in 1900 for her political activities, but through a curious relationship in prison with an assistant to the Interior Minister Von Plehve, Manya and Sergei Zubatov, head of the Moscow Secret Police, established the Jewish Independent Labor Party that would protect the Jewish workers from harassment as long as they limited themselves to labor issues.

In 1901, the party achieved many of its social and economic goals. However, soon after that, growing unemployment weakened its position and disenchantment by von Plehve brought a swift end to the party. At this time, von Plehve also began to agitate the masses against the Jews, and in 1903, the Kishinev Pogrom occurred. Soon after that, Manya's brother, knowing of the danger she was in, smuggled her into Palestine. She arrived on January 4, 1904. Thus, she was one of the first Second Aliyah immigrants who impacted on Jewish socialism in Palestine. From 1907 to 1920, she would become an outstanding leader of the Kibbutz Movement and the Histadrut Ha-Klalit (Fuchs 62-63).

In terms of ideology, Manya was to become a Zionist, but not just one who saw the need to transplant Jewish life from Russia to Palestine, but a strong believer in self-labor and collectivism. After her arrival, Manya, Nachum, Joshua Hankin, Olga (a midwife friend of Nachum's), and an Arab guide went on a six week tour of Palestine to study the geography and natural resources in order to determine how to develop a durable industrial foundation for the country. So important was that initial trip for her that she immediately became a Zionist: "She was seized by an extraordinary love of the country" (Near 25). After an extensive study of 23 of Baron de Rothschild's farms which she pronounced as totally bankrupt, she exclaimed, "As early as 1881, a pioneering wonderful, idealistic type of person came to Palestine, capable of minimal independent work, and now after they spent twenty-five years in the country, we found them completely reliant on ICA officials, lacking any faith in their enterprise, and employing Arab workers" (Fuchs 63-64).

In 1907, Manya joined a secret group, Bar Giora, which was organized by Yitchak Ben-Tzvi, the second President of Israel. Its goal was to protect the life and property of the Jewish people in Palestine using only Jewish guards. Most of the members of Bar Giora soon found their way to Sejera, where for the past seven years potential settlers had been trained by the JCA. Although she joined *Poale Zion*, Manya soon reached the conclusion that the 'conquest of labor', as propounded by both *Hapoel ha-Tzair* and *Poale Zion*, was doomed to failure. Manya Shohat was a socialist, but she also remained a maverick in her political ideas, one of which was that the only way to settle the country was by the establishment of collective settlements-"the collective provides the proletariat with its means of struggle." As noted earlier, that phrase summarized her socialist philosophy (Near 24).

After returning to Russia in order to take part in Jewish self-defense, she traveled to France and America to study colonization, visiting a number of religious communes before returning to Palestine. She then attempted to set up a carpenter cooperative, which failed. After that failures he joined the Bar Giora group.

At Sejera, Manya Shohat convinced the manager, Eliahu Krause to try an experiment where he contracted the labor on the farm to a small group of workers (the Bar Giora group) and turned over to them the seed, the tools, and the farm animals. Although he continued from time to time to give them some advice and lessons in agricultural science, they were allowed to organize and work the land in their own way. At the end of the year, the equipment was to be returned to the farm. In the event of profit, it was to be divided between the group of workers and the management. This became known as the Sejera

Collective. A small profit was made, unlike the previous years when more conventional methods of management were used (Near 25).

However, the Bar Giora group left Sejera and set up Ha-shomer, a self-defense group, but it still used the same method of organization when contracted in the moshavot (plural for farms) where it settled. This group made a similar arrangement with management to do a defined job for a year on any moshava where it existed. The workers worked together, produced together, and often lived together in many cases where such group contract labor was arranged. Its essence was communal production. This experiment, initiated by Manya Shohat, spread throughout the labor movement and became known as the kvutza (Near 25). Although the kvutza was different than the commune, which was marked by communal consumption, it became the popular collective means to settle the land to such an extent that, as mentioned earlier, there were five kvutzot and four defense groups by 1909. After a few years of conflict with management and other experiments, (described in the previous chapter), the term kvutza was the main concept used for collective work by groups until 1920, whereupon the term kibbutz entered the lexicon of the Second and Third Aliyot (Near 26).

At Sejera women achieved much. Although in her own reporting Manya never mentioned it, there had to be separate training farms in 1911 at Kinneret. This occurred because women in Um Juni (later Degania) were isolated in the kitchen and the laundry and expressed their deep dissatisfaction. This did not occur in Sejera, due to Manya's charisma, the sheer numbers of women in the group, and Krause's personality. Eventually Manya served as the treasurer of Merchavia and wrote to The Lovers of Zion in Russia that the kvutza needed another 2,000 francs, and then listed the balance of monies sent during that difficult year: "Surety Fund 4,000 francs; Arms 1,400 francs; Assistance Fund 1,300 francs; 11 horses 30,000 francs (one horse was shot in an Arab attack)" (Hoffman 90).

In 1914, women workers began to hold national meetings at Merchavia and the Women's Movement in Israel was established (Fuchs 76).

During World War I, Manya, her husband Israel Shohat, who had helped to organize the self-defense group ha-Shomer were deported with their two children, and with many others who did not have Turkish citizenship, to Bursa, Turkey. In 1919, they returned and lived with their two children in Palestine for the rest of their lives except for a brief time when she traveled to the U.S.A. to encourage aliyah.

In December 1919, when *Hapoel ha-Tzair* and *Poale Zion* established the The Histadrut's Workers' Council, it was decided that the future Women's Workers Council (Poalot) would have two representatives in the Council of the *Histadrut*. Manya Shohat was thus chosen to be a member of the Histadrut's Council. Manya was one of the two women, including Rachel Yanait, chosen of ten members from the newly formed *Achdut ha-Avodah* (Kurland 35). In 1930, Manya Shohat and Rachel Yanait, the wife of the second President of Israel, Yitzchak Ben Tzvi, established the Arab Jewish-Friendship League.

In 1948 Manya became a member of the pro-Soviet communist *Mapam* party. She is often called the Mother of the Kibbutz Movement and the collective settlement.

Manya Shohat died in 1961. On her death bed, she was quoted as saying about the Jezreel Valley:" I love you. I love every tree we planted, every clod of this earth (Hoffman 89).

# VII

## COMMENTS AND CONCLUSIONS

*"We are a people in whom the past endures, in whom the present is inconceivable without moments gone by."—Abraham Joshua Heschel*

The leadership of the pioneering democratic socialist movement in Palestine used five or six terms or concepts that symbolized their Zionism and Socialism. Ben Gurion for example continually referred to those chalutzim as doing the work of the Zionist movement and the Jewish people's by realizing the emancipation, redemption, and regeneration. The devotees to the pioneering socialism were idealists and the vital driving force in the general Zionist work, and "galvanized and strengthened the will to realization of the whole Zionist movement" (Ben Gurion Selections 23, 27).

Syrkin was intrigued by Moses Hess because he heralded socialist-Zionism not just Zionism, and for a good reason, since it was Hess who wrote that Judaism is not anti-social but is concerned with the salvation of mankind (not the individual). "The special calling of the Jew is to offer the world "revelations affecting the social-life sphere" (Syrkin, Maria 47). Syrkin himself thusly stated it: "A classless society and national sovereignty are the only means of completely solving the Jewish problem" (Syrkin 54).

Syrkin also believed that the Jewish Socialists made aliyah because they turned away from the position that protested the world oppressors and those who took up the mantle of vicarious nationalism. Syrkin and Dov Ber Borochov viewed their socialism as a last haven for the Jews whom liberalism had betrayed (Syrkin 54).

101

Berl Katznelson, along with Nachman Syrkin and Dov Ber Borochov, evolved the theory of 'non-proletarization', which was the denial of the ability of the Jewish people in the Diaspora to make the transition from lumpen proletariat to true working-class status (Shapira 13). Yitzchak Tabenkin and Berl Katznelson both believed in the development of socialism in Palestine as 'constructive socialism;' whereby, there would be the creation of the socialist society which would by-pass the capitalist economy, or eliminate it. Tabenkin saw the instrument of this occurring in En Harod designated as the 'country-wide' kibbutz and the colonel of the Kibbutz ha-Meuchad kibbutz movement. Since the Histadrut accepted Ein Harod as the instrument of 'constructive socialism' (by 1925) which had been laid as the foundation of the Palestinian Socialist-Zionism in the Second Aliyah with its utopian elements pragmatic solutions, the two leaders saw eye to eye that 'constructive socialism' was the original solution to the problems of the Socialist-Zionist existence in Palestine (Shapira 13; Near 145-146).

In Israel by Lewisohn, the author who toured the kvutzot, referred not to socialism but to communistic settlements that stood in no opposition to the industrialists and merchants in the towns, since they did not wish to impose their experimental adventures in new forms upon others. He stressed that they were not interested in the class struggle but were flexible in that they were primarily dedicated to building up Palestine through creative Jewish efforts and were prepared to sink both doctrine and practice into the demands of the ultimate supreme goal (Lewisohn 168).

A.D. Gordon was as an inspirational leader for the youth of the *kvutzot* and in the *Gedud ha-Avodah*, and his own ideology was literally tied to the 'religion of labor.' According to Gordon, the linking of 'The Land' and the Jewish people was a moral imperative. This concept also related directly to *Kibbush Avodah*, the 'conquest of labor' that which permeated the whole labor movement. The centrality of the kibbutz in some of the leaders' minds also lent itself to 'ideological collectivism.' This stood out in Tabenkin's approach to the kibbutz movement. This position stated that since the kibbutz was united in its means of settling the land in its culture and all political positions, its decision-making on all social and political issues must be represented as a single unified stand of the whole kibbutz.

Zweig in the *Israeli Worker* claimed that the State should not take over industry and that this demand of the bourgeois in Israel that the large complex of Histadrut industries should be taken over by the State was and is rejected and resented by the Socialist parties. Based on Palestinian Jewish socialist history, Zweig concluded that the Histadrut workers could do on a voluntary basis what the State did elsewhere. In 1963, the Histadrut-owned Koor group of industries accounted for 36% of the output building materials (Pruess 206). "We have voluntary collectives, cooperatives, *Kibbutzim* and *Moshavim*" (Zweig 275-276).

Therefore, as Zweig and the original pioneers and their leadership viewed it, the Jewish version of a Socialist society in Palestine and later in Israel was neither State socialism nor State capitalism. The democratic governance in the collectives and ultimate Industrial Democracy of the Histadrut certainly was based on the volunteerism to which Zweig refers.

In 1965, Dr. Walter Preuss wrote that in the labor community were 540 cooperative agricultural settlements with a total population of 200,000, and it would be impossible to appraise their contribution to the national economy solely on the basis of facts. He then adds that it goes far beyond that, for its political, social, and economic aspects have an impact on the all-around build-up of the social structure which cannot be raised in figures alone. He points out that in the kibbutz there can be a wide variety of agricultural and industrial branches in a single economic unit; and prophetically predicting, while looking back at the same time, that settlements permit experimentation and development of new forms of social life, some more collectivist and others more individualistic in character (Preuss 190-191).

The focus of this book has been on the young men and women pioneers of the first three Aliyot to Palestine between the years 1880-1924. In the forefront of the few thousand of those idealistic revolutionaries who had high expectations of creating the 'new man' and the 'new woman' were intellectual, spiritual, and pragmatic leaders who strove to develop a democratic and socialist settlement society in the barren and desolate Ottoman-ruled Palestine. The first groups of pioneers included young people who voluntarily participated in utopian communal living and organized democratic systems of governance. These young idealists created the social experiments that eventually did succeed to establish a socialist settlement society. The leaders such as David Ben Gurion, Berl Katznelson, Manya Shohat, A.D. Gordon, Yitzchak Tabenkin, and Dov Ber Borochov led the way socially and politically while setting personal examples as idealists who for decades lived austere and pragmatic lives in order to set an example for how their peers could achieve democratic and socialist goals.

The impact of those pioneers from the three waves of immigration, 1880-1924, is still being felt today in the modern Israeli society, and the expectations for institutional decision-making to contain elements of social justice and democratic means to establish such policy is still not only relevant, but at a very high level on the part of the new generation of literary, social, political, and legal-minded figures.

# AFTERWARD

Since 1980, the *kibbutzim* have not had uniformity. Only some are pure, and many have different degrees of private property and management. One of the many causes for change was that the kibbutz movement secularity, which compelled religious Zionists had to find their own *klbbutzim*. Immediately after the establishment of the State, the demographics of the Jewish community rapidly changed and the proportion of residents from Muslim countries increased dramatically. These people, if not pious, had great respect and love for the traditions of their families and were antagonistic to the population of the *kibbutzim* which had much higher standards of living than they did as unskilled workers. They were also antagonistic toward the secular-oriented communalism of kibbutz life.

This factor and others lead to the overall loss of political clout of the Kibbutz Movement and the Histadrut. Thus, politics and the weakening of the volunteerism, self-sacrificing nature of the Kibbutz Movement's population led to major changes of the socialist sector of Israeli society.

In some cases, however, as with Amos Oz, and other youth of the Kibbutz Movement who were returning soldiers in 1967, they held to the feeling that it was morally wrong to occupy conquered lands. However, this was expressed by only a tiny minority of the country's population, and even only represented the young idealists of the United Kibbutz Movement, not the generation of Yitzchak Tabenkin, and such government ministers as Yigal Allon who had grown up in the left wing Palmach of Achdut Avodah. The gulf between the older generation and the younger one was the distance between *shell-shocked* and *ectasy*. The New Left never developed there, nor did a student revolt break out. For the small numbers of young left-wing returning soldiers, warfare was seen as "filthy." As for participatory democracy it already existed in the kibbutz every week at the General Meeting or when one took an extra turn milking cows. As for Revolution, it was a yawn, unlike in France, Mexico, and the U.S.A. that in a similar fashion was populated by Jewish youth who were children of their parents' Leftist backgrounds (Goremberg 88).

In an article posted on September 21, 2009 in the Newsletter of Ameinu, the Progressive Labor Zionist Organization in the United States, Leonard Fein scorched the Kibbutz Movement by calling it 'comatose." He claimed in a fashion that startled some of his readers that there were only twenty *kibbutzim* that had not used privatization as a means for change. He was especially critical of the kibbutz movement because Kibbutz Ein Harod privatized in 2009. For Fein, this was the straw that broke the back of the movement's ideological struggle to reach the expectations of the first three *Aliyot*. In the early 1920's, Ein Harod had been the largest and most ideological of the early kibbutzim. For example, Henry Near, a foremost kibbutz movement historian, wrote in his book The Kibbutz Movement Volume I, which was published in 2007 by the Littman Library of Jewish Civilization (Portland Oregon), that in the 1930's, the women members demanded that one-third of all places on the kibbutz's committees be reserved for women (367). Thus, Leonard Fein and many other Labor Zionists have become critical of the demise of the socialist democratic tranformative settlement society established by the Second and Third *Aliyot*.

However, other writers such as Gary Brenner and Jo-Ann Mort in their book Our Hearts Invented the Place have unequivocally stated that there are at least forty pure *kibbutzim*. The criteria for determining ideological purity was that they have retained the socialist and democratic institutions of the kibbutz of the 1920's. Privatization features such as private ownership of vehicles and private ownership of kibbutz housing do not exist in those *kibbutzim,* nor is there the selling or renting of buildings on non-agricultural kibbutz land for homes or for private enterprise. The lack of collective management of work and the key privatization element of wage differentiation is not part of any of the pure *kibbutzim.*

The continuity of collective living including the entire management of their own branches of agriculture and industry, the social and cultural community activities created together as a collective, and work being assigned by work coordinators and committees still exists in the pure *kibbutz*. In their book, Brenner and Mort listed some wealthier *kibbutzim such* as Gan Smuel that was on the top of the list of "pure" *kibbutzim*. Hazor, where they themselves have lived, was *placed* in the middle of the pack of 287 *kibbutzim* because it still had the collective responsibility for the members' health, education, and welfare; and its members believed that they were making the world a better place. However, it was not considered one of the forty pure kibbutzim. Gesher Haziv (and others) was analyzed as a municipality, and was at the bottom ideologically. In that regard, however, the positive outcome for some *kibbutzim* such as Gesher Haziv was that the young sons and daughters who had left the *kibbutzim* in droves in the 1980's were now returning to live in a community, not a kibbutz, privatized but yet physically very close to the original kibbutz. In addition, there were many urban collectives and communes in major urban areas that were established by young people, non-profit groups fulfilling the social justice goals of the first *chalutzim*. In many people's eyes, they represented the reawakening of the Israeli Left. Many of these groups had sprung from youth movements; and in some cases new *kibbutzim* have been founded. This new social movement of the Twenty-First Century was following in the footsteps of grandparents and great grandparents.

Henry Near in his kibbutz movement's history pointed out that in 1939 there were "twenty-five thousand people in 117 collective groups ranging from the northern border of Palestine to the northern approaches of the Negev and from the Mediterranean to the new settlements along the Jordan Valley." There were also in reserve one hundred thousand people in Palestine and in the Diaspora who were in the pioneering youth movements. He stated in the last pages of his book The Kibbutz Movement, Volume I that there were no illusions in 1939 about the dangers they faced, but "whatever the course of the struggle to come, they were convinced of the rightness of their cause" (Near 398-399).

However, Daniel Gavron in his book The Kibbutz claimed that the kibbutz members knew that whatever its faults the kibbutz system worked. They knew that their families' welfare would be secure. In 2000, Gavron wrote: "that was no longer true" (3). The situation changed due to economic and social issues revolving around the movement to a new market economy by the country, and the lack of subsidies from the right wing Likud government after 1977, as well as the individualism which sprung from the desire to withdraw from the volunteer mentality of the veteran *chalutzim* of the first three *Aliyot*. In an article in the Forward, May 6, 2011, Nathan Jeffay made the point that "until 1985 under the rule of socialist parties, Israel was known for strong government intervention in the economy with a robust social welfare policy and a highly unionized workforce. However, responding to poor economic performance and high inflation, the government in that year enacted an Economic Stabilization Plan that cut public spending, gave the business sector a large leadership role, and paved the way for further market-oriented structural reforms" (Jeffay 10). The next year privatization did begin and to this date, 90 governmental entities have been privatized.

During the years when Bejamin Netanyahu was Finance Minister, he cut income support by 30%, and union membership plunged from the 85% before 1985 to 30% today. After Israel joined the Organization for Economic Cooperation and Development, the group representing the world's strongest economies published that Israel's poverty was almost twice that of the average of the other 33 countries in the group (19.9 % of the population compared to 10.9 %) and that although the percentage of people living in poor families went up to 25% from 23.7% in the last year, its welfare spending of only 16 % of its budget was five percentage points below the OECD countries' average. One OECD expert stated that Israel needs to shift the composition of social spending toward more cost-effective benefits and increase investment in that area. According to the evaluation by Israel's own National Insurance Institute, there was an "exacerbation" of inequality, and that the socio-economic policy is on a course which is not sustainable. Thus, the ideologically democratic and socialist mentality and policies that had only extended the impact of the Histadrut and the *kibbutzim* on the country until the mid-1980's are being viewed once more as needed, by not only the historical writers of the socialist transformative pioneering society, but also by modern socio-economic national and international experts.

There are recent signs that the renewal of such institutions and movements of the veteran socialist-democratic society have been rejuvenated in this Twenty-First Century, adding pragmatic leadership to their roles and using at times the old formulas of negotiating and threatening strikes as the Histadrut does; and as the developments of the new democratic collectives and quasi socialist societies in the heavily populated urban areas have created.

In 2011, university students, graduates of Israeli youth movements, and young army veterans who view warfare as "filthy" are leading a revolt. They have already developed the non-profits that manifest Jewish social values and they have begun to revolt in Jerusalem and other major cities. They are revolting against anti-democratic loyalty oaths, religious and ethnic discrimination, the seizing of and the occupation of Palestinian homes and lands and the gaps between the rich and the poor. They are opposed to policies that run counter to their prophetic social justice traditions, and act as their leaders and all of the Jewish democratic socialist movements once did in Israel.

# GLOSSARY

Achdut ha-Avodah—Labor Unity. It was the movement in 1919 to unite two parties which enabled the United Labor Movement to establish the Histadrut (General Federation of Labor).

Achadut ha-Avodah in 1919. The first socialist party of the new era which combined it and Poale Zion was Mapai to form the Labor Party, established in 1930.

Achdut ha-Avodah; The left wing party which split from the Israeli Labor Party, Mapai, in the 1940's.

Aliyah—Immigration to Israel. It translates literally as "going up"–to Jerusalem in historical terms. May be used as a wave of immigration such as The First Aliyah 1880-1904.

Aliyot—Plural of Aliyah

BILU—The letters stood for the Hebrew term Bet Yaakov Lechu Ulnechu The House of Jacob You Shall Go and We Shall Go. The First Aliyah pioneers were part of BILU which did intend to settle the land.

Bund—Jewish Socialists who were anti-Zionists in Russia and Poland. They were essentially wiped out in the 1930's but did exist later in USA. They spoke Yiddish since related more to the country in which they lived not the goal of reaching Palestine.

Birobidjhan—The Jewish Collective which Stalin set up in Siberia. It was closed in 1958 by Khruschev.

Bolshevik—The Social Democratic Party which Lenin called in 1917, Bolsheviki meaning the majority, even though it was relatively the minority party in comparison to the other Social Democratic wing (Mensheviks). From the beginning, its position was anti-Zionist.

Chalutzim—Pioneers (masculine).

Chalutzot—Pioneers (feminine).

Chevrat Ovdim—Cooperative Association of Labor. All the cooperatives of the Histadrut united into one cooperative.

Eretz Israel— The Land of Israel.

Gedud ha-Avodah—The Labor Battalion which was developed through the ideology of Yosef Trumledor and A. D. Gordon. It contracted with the British to build roads and work in stone quarries during the Third Aliyah (1919-1924). It was based on the Tolstoyan ideology of Jewish settlement leaders such as Joseph Trumpledor and A. D. Gordon. Its members were in many cases members of the first collectives, kibbutzim and kvutzot (See below).

Gush Emunim—The Bloc of the Faithful. Historically this is the name given to the Settler Movement after 1970.

Habonim—The Builders. This is an existing Labor Zionist Youth Movement that united with the Labor Zionist movement in the USA presently known as Ameinu. Its parent movement was Poale Zion.

Hagshama Atzmit—Self Realization. This motto was used often by the pioneers and left wing Zionist youth movements.

Hamashbir—The Crisis. A Consumer Cooperative established in 1916 to allow workers to buy food for their collectives in volume and at cheaper prices. Later it also became a Marketing Cooperative.

Hapoel ha-Tzair—The Young Worker. This was one of the two socialist political parties in the Second Aliyah period which eventually was united to form the Labor Movement's Achadut ha-Avodah in 1919.

Haganah—The self-defense organization of the 1930's. Because of riots by the Arabs in Jerusalem and in other cities where Jews were living, it was established in 1920 under the control of the Histadrut. In 1921, when the urban riots occurred, the word 'hagana' was heard in the streets.

Ha-Ichud Ha-Kvutzot Ve ha-Kibbutzim—The Kibbutz Movement associated with Mapai established in 1930 and the leading party in the First Knesset (Parliament).

Hashomer ha-Tzair—The left wing youth movement which was not part of the urban labor movement settlement ideology but whose members settled kibbutzim. It was more democratic in many ways than the Gedud, and was part of the Kibbutz Artzi kibbutz movement.

Ha-Shomrim—The Guards—This group started out as pioneers who guarded kibbutzim but also established their own kibbutzim as did Bar Giora before them.

Hechalutz—The Pioneer. It was originally the Poale Zion Youth Movement in Europe but other youth movements used it for training farms and granting immigration certificates so it became an umbrella organization. It was established in 1917.

Heder—The classroom in which Jewish youth in Europe learned Hebrew, Yiddish, Torah, Talmud, and Jewish Literature.

Histadrut ha-Klalit—The General Federation of Labor established at a 1920 Conference by representatives of the entire Socialist-Zionist Settlement Movement.

Jewish National Fund or Keren Kayemet—The organization of the Zionist Movement which bought the land and leased it to the farmers in the settlements.

Hovevei Zion—Ostensibly, it was a Russian Jewish organization with its center in Odessa. It was established by Leon Pinsker and Moses Lilenblum in 1889 to assist Jewish colonization to Palestine. It eventually spread to Romania Austria, Germany, England, and the United States.

Jewish Legion—This military brigades which were part of the British Army in World War I and were later recruited in the 1920's by Zeev Jabotinsky to defend Jews in Palestine.

Keren Ha Yasod—The Palestine Foundation Fund. It helped to administer monies for tools, farm animals, and seed for the pioneers.

Kibbutz—Consumer and productive collectives. This terminology was used by the 1920's. The term was permanently used by the early 1920's when it became obvious that collectives much larger than the kvutzot had crystallized in size and ideology and were stable societies in Palestine.

Kibbush Avodah—The 'conquest of labor.' Also translated as 'Jewish labor' This expression was famous in the left wing collective agricultural societies and movements from the early days and connoted that if Jews could successfully farm the land the spiritual aspects of that conquest of labor would fulfill them as a people.

Kibbutz Ha Meuchad. The Kibbutz Movement which arose the aftermath of the Third Aliyah and was parallel later in in the 1940's to the political party Achdut ha-Avodah.

Kvutza—Group. They were small communal working groups whose members contracted to work for a defined time or objective. They were agricultural communal groups which became social experiments at the beginning of the Second Aliyah. The kvutzot were productive cooperatives. At the early stages, they worked for the Jewish Colonial Association on a moshava (private farm for families with individual plots). The farms often were training farms which could be sold to Jewish farmers after the pioneers of the Second Aliyah were trained. Historically the kvutzot were the backbone of the socialist agricultural societies and lead the way in the 'conquest of the land' during the Second and Third Aliyot.

Kibbutz Artzi—The National Kibbutz Movement of Ha-Shomer ha-Tzair.

Kvutzot Poalim—A group of workers who did not have the capital to own land, farm animals, or tools, but contracted all those necessary items in order to work the land.

Likud—The right wing Zionist Party which came to power in 1977.

Mapai—The Labor Party established in 1930 which in 1949 became the leading political party of the First Coalition Government (garnered 45 Knesset seats).

Menshevik or Mensheviki—The Minority Party is a literal translation, but the Mensheviks were the majority of the Social Democrats in Russia who followed Martov's program before the Party's name was changed (by Lenin) in April 1917 to the Communist Party. The Bolsheviks who were in the minority under Lenin became the majority by name only and created the Revolution and the government of the Soviet Union.

Moshav and Moshavim (plural)—Small settlement developed for family units with wide measure of cooperation in marketing and purchasing. They were first established during the beginning of the Third Aliyah (1919). Nahalal was the first one established and the most famous, but soon there were many others. Some pioneers viewed it as a threat to the collectives of the Second Aliyah.

Moatza—Literally, it means Counsel. In this context it refers to the Histadrut's executive branch. Parties were given representation depending on the voting percentage that each party received. Women also insisted and won places on the first Histadrut Moatza through the choosing of two women from Moatzet Ha Poalot (The Women's Workers Council) On the original Moatza, there were 21 members.

Norodnaya Volya (The Peoples Will)—Anti-Czarist organization that identified with the peasants and was strong in the 1870's but soon became anarchistic and had diminishing influence after the assassination of Czar Alexander in 1881.

Pale of Settlement or The Pale—This refers to the area in the Russian Empire in the Nineteenth and early Twentieth Centuries to which the Jewish citizens were restricted.

Poale Zion—Workers of Zion. Socialist (mainly Marxist) Zionist Party. It originated in the Diaspora at the turn of the century. It became the leading branch in the labor movement from 1906-1919. In Palestine it disbanded to become one with Ha-Poel ha-Tzair, forming Achdut ha-Avodah. In 1920, a minority split off into Left Poale Zion and became an independent political party throughout the entire world.

Seimists—From the Polish "Seim" meaning Parliament. The non-Marxist socialist Jewish group was in contact with the Social Revolutionaries and sought national Jewish autonomy with a Parliament. Officially it was called the Jewish Socialist Labor Party.

# REFERENCES

Baratz, Joseph. *Village by the Jordan*. New York: Schulsinger Bros. Linotyping and Publishing Company, 1957.

Becker, Aharon. *Histadrut Faces the Future*. New York: National Committee for Labor Israel, 1962.

Ben Gurion, David. *Rebirth: The Destiny of Israel*. New York: Philosophical Library, 1954.

Ben Gurion, David. *Selections*. New York: Labor Zionist Organization of America, 1948.

Ber Borachov, Dov. *Nationalism and the Class Struggle*. New York: Poale Zion-Zeire Zion of America, 1937.

"Berl Katznelson 1877-1944" www.jafi.org, *The Jewish Agency*.

Berlin, Isaiah. *The Power of Ideas*. New York: Crown Publishers, 2002.

Chaim Weizmann: on his Centenary, 1874-1974. New York: Youth and Education Department of the Jewish National Fund, 1974.

Dannhauser, Warner. "A Home of One's Own." *New York Times* 14 Jul. 2008: 1.

Diament, Carol. Ed. *Zionism: the Sequel*. New York: Hadassah, 1998.

Eban, Abba. *Heritage: Civilization and the Jews*. New York: Summit Books, 1984.

Elon, Amos. *Founders and Sons*. New York: Penquin Books, 1971.

Fein, Leonard. "An Experiment That, for a Time, Did Not Fail." Ameinu Newsletter 21 Sept. 2009:1

Frank, Ben. *A Jewish Travel Guide to Russia and the Ukraine* Gretna Louisiana:Pelican Publishing Company Inc., 2000.

Frank, Ivan, C. *Israel The Dream*: What Then, What Now. Pittsburgh, Pennsylvania: 2007.

Fromkin, David. *A Peace to End All Peace.* New York: Henry Holt and Company, 2001.

Fuchs, Esther, Ed. *Israeli Women's Studies*. New Brunswick, New Jersey: Rutgers University Press, 2005.

Goetthel, Richard, J.H. *Zionism*. Philadelphia: The Jewish Publication Society, *1914.*

Gordon, A.D. *Selected Essays.* Trans. Frances Burnice. New York: League for Labor Israel, 1938.

Granovsky, Abraham. *Land Policy in Palestine*. New York: Bloch Publishing Company, 1940.

Hapern, Ben. *Labor's Role in Palestine. New York:* Shulsinger Linotyping and Publishing Company.

Hoffman, Lawrence. *A Spiritual Travel Guide*. Woodstock, Vermont: Jewish Lights Publishing, 1998.

Katznelson, Berl. *The Kvutza*. (Hebrew). Tel Aviv: 1924.

Kirshner, Israel."The Kibbutz Sheds Socialism." *New York* Times 27 Aug. 2007: A1.

Kurland, Samuel. *Cooperative Palestine*. New York: Sharon Books, 1947.

*Labor Zionist Handbook* New York: Poale Zion-Zeire Zion of America, 1934.

Lewisohn, Ludwig. *Israel*. New York: Boni and Livright, 1925.

Malkosh, Noah. *Histadrut in Israel. Tel Aviv:* National Committee for Labor Israel, 1961

Merlstein, M. *Berl Katznelson*. (Yiddish). Latin America Department of the Histadrut, 1959.

Mniewski, Myra and Pollack, Chana. 'Women's Work" The Jewish Forward. New York: 20 Feb. 2009: 17.

Near, Henry, *The Kibbutz Movement Vol. I.* Portland Oregon:

The Litman Library of Jewish Civilization, 2007.

*Oz, Amos. A Tale of Love and Darkness.* Trans. Nicholas de_Lange. Orlando Florida: Harcourt Inc., 2003.

Preuss, Walter. *The Labor Movement in Israel.* Jerusalem: AhavaPress, 1965.

Ramon, Einat. "Jewish Identity." New York: *Ameinu Newsletter*, 2008.

Reuvsky, Abraham. *The Histadrut.* New York: League for Labor Palestine, 1938.

Rolef, Susan "Yitzchak Tabenkin." *Encylopedia Judaica 2$^{nd}$ Edition, Vol. I.* 2007.

Rophie, Annie. "A Light on the Fence." *Jerusalem Report* Mar. 47: 18.

Shapira, Anita. *Berl* New York: Cambridge University Press, 1984.

Sleznick, Yuri. *The Jewish Century.* Princeton, New Jersey: Princeton University Press, 1956.

Syrkin, Maria. *Socialist Zionist.* New York: Herzl Press and_Sharon Books, 1961.

*"The History of Zionism."* www.Zionism-Israel.com.

"The Land Question in Palestine." *Zionism and Israel News Encyclopedic Dictionary*, www.zionism-israel.com/dic/Land 9 Jul. 08: 1

*The Socialist International and Zionism.* New York:_Poale Zion-Zeire_Zion, 1933.

Vlavianos, Basil. Ed. *The Struggle for Tomorrow*. New York: Arts Inc., 1953.

Wolfe, Bertram. *To the Finland Station.* New York: Doubleday and Company, 1940.

Wolfe, Robert. *Remember to Dream.* New York: The Jewish Radical Education Project, 1994.

Weisgal, Meir. Ed. *Theodore Herzl: A Memorial*. New York: The New Palestine, 1929.

Yarmolinsky, Avraham. *Road to Revolution*. New York: Colllier Books, 1962.

Zweig, Fernyndad. *The Israeli Worker*, New York: Herzl; Press, 1959.

## ABOUT THE AUTHOR

Dr. Ivan Frank is a veteran educator of over fifty years experience both in the United States and Israel. He lived in kibbutz in Israel in the late 1950s, and again with his family from 1977-1982. He holds a Ph.D. in the International Development Education Program, with an emphasis on education and social movements. His M.A. is in Modern European History (1972). His Ph.D. dissertation was written in Israel and completed after its defense in January of 1981 in Pittsburgh. He is a member of Ameinu, the progressive Labor Zionist Movement and the Steering Committee of the prominent pro-Israel, pro-peace group J Street. His B.A. is in Education with majors in History and Social Sciences (1963). He has taught at Ben Gurion University and at the Regional College of the Negev, as well as organizing a seminar on kibbutz life for kibbutz Nachal Oz, and worked for the Histatdrut in Israel training Africans and Asians in the development of Labor and Cooperative movements. He has written four books on Israel, one historical, covering 1880-2007 and three on kibbutz ideology and education. He lived in the second urban collective in Israeli History for four years. He teaches courses for the Osher Program on Israeli History, Israeli Current Events and the Development of Socialism in Israel at University of Pittsburgh and Carnegie Mellon University. His book Children in Chaos (Praeger, 1992) is included in the collection at the Carnegie Library in New York City, and the University of Pittsburgh Library.

He resides in Pittsburgh.